AF808160

The Fresh Start Credit Fix

Understanding Credit and Your Credit Report

Table of Contents

Foreword

To the many who grapple with the challenge of building and maintaining good credit, this book is for you. Your journey, often hidden behind closed doors, is one of silent struggle and perseverance. In a world where creditworthiness can feel like a measure of personal success, it is easy to feel overwhelmed and discouraged. Yet, amidst these trials lies the potential for growth and transformation. This book is not merely a collection of financial tips but a testament to the strength found in facing one's financial fears head-on. It is about turning setbacks into comebacks and financial turmoil into triumph.

Understanding credit is more than just numbers and scores; it is about gaining the knowledge and tools to navigate a system that seems daunting at first glance. Each chapter of this book is crafted with care, designed to guide you through the complexities of credit, from the basics of building a credit history to the nuances of repairing and maintaining it. The path to good credit is often winding and fraught with obstacles, but with perseverance and the right guidance, it is undoubtedly navigable. This book aims to light the way, offering hope and practical advice to those who feel lost in the credit maze.

I have written this book with the belief that everyone deserves a second chance, and your credit history is not an indelible mark of your financial capabilities. It reflects a moment in time, not a lifetime sentence. Here, you will find stories of individuals who, like you, faced their financial dilemmas and emerged stronger. These narratives are shared not just for empathy but for empowerment, illustrating that change is possible and within reach. Let these stories inspire you to take the reins of your financial journey, transforming your relationship with money and credit.

As you turn these pages, remember that your journey to good credit is a step towards greater financial freedom and stability. This book is a companion in your quest, providing not just advice but also understanding and support. Financial wellness is a holistic journey that encompasses more than just credit scores; it is about building a foundation for a prosperous and secure future. With each chapter, you are not just reading a book; you are taking a step towards reclaiming your financial independence and shaping a future where your dreams and aspirations are not hindered by credit challenges.

Dedication

To my cherished family,

This book, a labor of love and persistence, is dedicated to you, for you have been the pillars of strength and resilience in my life, especially through the tumultuous years of personal struggle. Your unwavering belief and steadfast support have been the guiding stars in my darkest nights, illuminating the path towards fulfillment and success. In every step of this long journey, through setbacks and victories, your love has been a constant source of comfort and courage. Your faith in me, even when I faltered, helped me stand firm and keep moving forward, transforming challenges into stepping stones.

Your sacrifices have not gone unnoticed, for each one has laid the foundation for this book. To my partner, whose patience and kindness are boundless, you have been my rock, offering solace and strength in equal measure. To my daughter, whose laughter and joy have been my greatest motivators, you have taught me the true value of perseverance and hope. Your ability to see light in the face of adversity has inspired the very essence of this work, teaching me that with love and support, overcoming even the most daunting financial obstacles is possible.

To the wider circle of relatives and friends who have been part of this journey, your encouragement and belief in my vision have been invaluable. This book is more than just a guide to credit repair; it is a testament to the power of enduring familial bonds and shared dreams. Your presence in my life has been a gift of immeasurable worth, and this achievement is as much yours as it is mine. Thank you for being my sanctuary, my audience, and my inspiration.

INTRODUCTION

"Ever wondered why your credit score is like your financial fingerprint? It is unique, it tells a story, and its got the power to open doors or slam them shut."

Buckle up because we are diving into the world of credit in *"The Fresh Start Credit Fix,"* and trust me, it is a journey you will not want to miss. We are not talking about mind-numbing numbers here; we are talking about your financial story, the ups, the downs, and the in-betweens - all neatly packed into what we call your credit report.

You know how they say your past shapes your future? Well, in the financial world, your credit is like the backstage pass to your financial show. From snagging that dream apartment to landing a killer interest rate on your dream car, credit is the unsung hero of your financial escapades.

Now, about those mysterious credit reports. Think of them as your financial report card – a bit intimidating at first, but once you get the hang of it, a total game-changer. We are here to decode the secret language within those reports, revealing the tales they tell about your financial choices and misadventures.

Good credit, bad credit - it is not just about numbers on a scale. It is the hero and the villain in your financial saga. A stellar credit score? That is your golden ticket to better deals and opportunities. A not-so-stellar score? Time to face a few financial dragons. Stick with us as we unravel the drama and show you how to turn the plot in your favor.

So, kick back, relax, and get ready for a journey into the world of credit where learning meets laughter, and your financial empowerment takes center stage. Welcome to "The Fresh Start Credit Fix" – where your credit score is not just a number; it is your financial superhero cape. Let us do this!

CHAPTER 1.
BASICS OF CREDIT

Welcome to the credit universe – where financial possibilities and responsibilities intersect. In this chapter, we will embark on a journey through the fundamentals of credit, decoding its definition, exploring its rich history, understanding its purpose, uncovering the perks of good credit, and shedding light on the regulatory guardian – the Fair Credit Reporting Act.

Definition and History of Credit

Credit, in a nutshell, is a financial lifeline. It is the trust given to someone to repay borrowed money. Picture this: ancient civilizations engaged in credit-like systems, trusting each other to trade goods on a promise. Fast forward to today, and credit is the currency of financial dreams. It is the tool that empowers individuals to make significant purchases and investments.

Credit is like a promise with a purpose. It is when someone lends you money, trusting you will pay it back. Think of it as a friend spotting you cash until your next payday. In the grand scheme of finance, it is your ticket to making big moves, even when your wallet is playing hard to get.

The concept of credit has existed since ancient times, with records of merchant lenders providing loans with interest rates dating back to early Mesopotamian and Egyptian societies thousands of years ago. However, more formalized consumer credit systems really began to take shape in the early 20th century.

In the early 1900s, many consumer goods like furniture, stoves, sewing machines and early automobiles began being sold on an installment credit basis. This allowed consumers unable to afford big ticket items to incrementally pay off purchases over weeks or months with interest. By the 1920s, department stores, gas stations and other retailers issued charge cards to select customers.

The onset of the Great Depression saw default rates rise as millions lost jobs and could not repay debts. The first modern credit bureaus emerged by reporting these defaults and tracking consumer payment histories to help lenders mitigate risk. Legislation like the Truth in Lending Act (TILA) then attempted to standardize how credit costs were communicated to consumers with regulations on terms like APR.

Bank-issued general-purpose credit cards like BankAmericard, later Visa, began in 1958. This was followed by Mastercard in 1966 which marked the genesis of revolving credit cards tied to payment card networks still used prominently today. Credit scoring models like the FICO score were first introduced in 1989 as a standardized way of determining consumer credit risk.

Over time, credit availability and types expanded greatly. In 1950 consumer credit outstanding sat at just $8.1 billion but topped $4 trillion by 2022. Today consumers have diverse credit options spanning credit cards, payday loans, mortgages, student loans, car financing and more. Credit bureaus maintain detailed credit reports charting an individual's obligations, balances, and payment history with this access to credit.

While credit was more tightly controlled and less available to average consumers for much of the early 20th century, perspectives and regulation shifted dramatically starting in the 1970s and 1980s. This credit deregulation removed many previous restrictions and limits in lending.

Banks and retailers rapidly expanded offerings like general purpose credit cards, home equity lines of credit, and financing for cars and education expenses that let consumers borrow substantial sums. Lending criteria also loosened significantly, bringing credit access to a wider demographic.

This combination sparked an unprecedented escalation in household debt levels over the following decades. By the early 2000s, credit card debt alone exceeded $700 billion with the average American holding four to five open cards. Many consumers began heavily relying on readily available revolving credit and accumulating problematic balances mired in interest fees.

The subprime mortgage crisis hitting in 2007 marked a turning point with reexamination of loose credit norms. As millions defaulted on risky home loans and unaffordable debt burdens, regulators again tightened criteria for borrowers to qualify for additional credit. Consumer advocacy groups also pushed for more transparency in communicating fees, rates and risks upfront.

Today's credit landscape balances this push and pull between open access and responsible lending. Credit is more available than ever before to consumers across income levels. But factors like payment history, existing debts and credit scores now play a heightened role for lenders in determining approval odds, limits and terms. Most experts advise maintaining modest debt loads and diligently making payments on time.

The Purpose of Credit, Simply Put

At its core, credit is just a measure of trust between you and lending institutions. It allows lenders to evaluate how reliably you have paid back money borrowed in the past, and subsequently determine how creditworthy you are to take on more debt now or in the future.

Those with very high credit scores are considered highly dependable borrowers who lenders compete fiercely to do business with by offering the best terms. On the other hand, those with poor scores are seen as higher risk and either denied loans or credit cards outright, or extended subprime terms like very high interest rates.

The obvious advantage goes to those who faithfully obey the "credit rules" over time and build robust credit histories which unlock easier access to financing that makes major life goals affordable.

The Perks of Strong Credit

Maintaining a great credit standing bestows plenty of tempting privileges you should not miss out on. For one, favorable interest rates that could save thousands of dollars in interest payments alone when it comes time for major purchases like buying a house or a car. Even daily expenses like groceries, insurance premiums or utility bills can become markedly cheaper with a good credit score qualifying you for the top rewards credit cards or programs.

Beyond the direct dollars and cents, a high credit score just makes life easier and offers increased financial flexibility. You do not have to worry as much before a big expense because lenders are more willing to work with you. Things just seem to magically get approved thanks to your rating, and should an emergency arise, you have quick access to credit you may desperately require.

Different types of credit serve as valuable tools in enhancing your credit score, contingent upon consistent and punctual payments. These avenues include:

1. **Single-payment/service credit:** This pertains to services where payment is made every month, typically without accruing interest. Common examples encompass utility bills and phone bills.

2. **Installment credit:** Under this category, a loan is repaid through a predetermined series of payments, usually with interest. Instances of installment credit encompass student loans and car loans.

3. **Revolving credit:** This form allows for multiple purchases within a defined credit limit. Repayment occurs periodically, typically requiring a minimum payment, with interest applied if the full balance is not

cleared each billing cycle. Credit cards and lines of credit are prime illustrations of revolving credit options.

Regulation and the Law (Fair Credit Reporting Act) and its Purpose

In the battle for credit justice, the Fair Credit Reporting Act (FCRA) is your mighty weapon. This landmark federal law governs the credit reporting industry and spells out your rights when it comes to your credit files. It was passed in 1970 to promote accuracy, fairness, and privacy for consumers interacting with credit reporting agencies.

The FCRA gives you rights to dispute errors on your reports, requires credit bureaus to thoroughly investigate disputes in a reasonable time frame, and restricts who can access your credit reports. It mandates that credit bureaus have procedures in place for correcting inaccuracies promptly.

This law is the framework that makes it possible for consumers to compel credit bureaus to fix reporting mistakes that unjustly lower scores. Without the FCRA's critical consumer protections, you would have no power to challenge errors and oversight by the big credit agencies.

Knowing the specific provisions of the FCRA gives you a better shot at successfully repairing credit damage when you find misinformation on your reports - which 1 in 5 Americans unfortunately do.

Understanding APR (Annual Percentage Rate)

When a person takes out a loan from any source, one is likely to come across the term Annual Percentage Rate (APR). But what does it mean and why is it important? APR stands for an annual percentage rate, which is technically the cost of borrowing expressed as a yearly interest rate. It encompasses not just the rate of interest on the loan but also other expenses including origination fees, points, or closing costs.

How Does APR Work?

Suppose you are shopping for a loan and you find two options: Loan A with an APR of 5% and Loan B with an APR of 7%. At first sight, Loan A might look more attractive because it has a lower APR. However, there are other considerations apart from this such as fees, repayment schedule, and the term of the loan.

The exact formula for computing APR often varies depending on some factors such as the type of credit instrument and specific conditions applied in each case. Nevertheless, ordinarily speaking, APR considers interest rates together with all extra costs associated with loans. Therefore, lenders are required by law to disclose this information so that their customers can make well-informed choices as far as borrowing is concerned. Understanding what goes into calculating your annual percentage rate matters because it enables you to compare different types of loans based on their true cost of borrowing. By looking at APR alone you have an idea of how much total interest payments over a lifetime as well as fee due will be which will enable you to decide upon the affordability of alternative credit products applicable to your financial situation.

Example:

Suppose you have received two credit card offers:

- Card A has an annual fee of $50 and its Annual Interest Rate (APR) is 18%.
- Card B has no annual fee but its Annual Interest Rate (APR) is 20%.

At first look, Card B may seem better since it does not incur maintenance charges annually. Nonetheless, after considering the annual fee along with the APR on Card B, you will find out that Card A is cheaper in terms of overall borrowing cost, particularly for those who revolve month by month.

A Deep Dive into the Fair Credit Reporting Act

As mentioned, the FCRA is your strongest ally in the battle for fair credit reporting. When your credit reports or scores suffer because of incorrect or outdated information, the FCRA requires credit bureaus and furnishers (the banks, lenders, and collection agencies that report your info) to follow strict guidelines around resolving inaccuracies.

The Key Protections of the FCRA Include:

The Right to Access Your Credit Reports and Scores - You have a right to request a copy of your credit report from each of the three major credit bureaus (Experian, Transunion, and Equifax) once per year as well as purchase up-to-date credit scores. This allows you to monitor for errors and negative items that may unjustly drop your score.

The Right to Dispute Inaccurate or Incomplete Information - You have the right to start a dispute process directly with the credit bureaus and original furnishers to correct factual inaccuracies on your reports related to identification information, account status, payment history, outstanding debt etc. This is one of the most important tools used during credit repair to remove damaging items that lower your score.

Response and Investigation Requirements for Disputes - Once you submit a dispute, there are strict legal time limits that the bureaus and furnishers must adhere to. Credit bureaus typically have 30 calendar days to investigate the dispute and respond to you on the status of the reinvestigation efforts. The FCRA forces them to put manpower towards ensuring accuracy.

Furnisher Requirements to Report Accurate Information - Lenders, collection agencies, and any other party reporting your payment info must use reasonable procedures to ensure the data they send to credit bureaus is complete and up-to-date. They have additional requirements around timely responses to disputes opened through the bureaus about the information they furnished. If not reasonably accurate or timely, they face penalties under the FCRA.

Understanding these rights under federal law prepares you to catch issues early and take action to fix them before lasting damage is done to your credit standing. The FCRA brings accountability to such a far-reaching system.

The Standard in Credit Scoring – FICO / Vantage

FICO, the name for Fair Isaac Corporation, is a data analytics firm that specializes in predictive analytics and decision management solutions. Established by engineer Bill Fair and mathematician Earl Isaac in 1956, FICO has become an essential aspect of credit scoring and is recognized globally as the major provider of credit scoring models.

In the mid-20th century, when Fair and Isaac decided to change how lenders assess creditworthiness, FICO began its journey. It was their original work that resulted in the establishment of the first ever credit scoring system using statistical models that would evaluate lending risks on individual borrowers based on their previous credit history.

Since then, FICO has evolved over time by incorporating additional data sources into its credit scores, using advanced analytical methods and industry-specific insights. Worldwide, thousands of lenders use FICO scores to assist them make appropriate decisions regarding granting loans to customers or businesses.

Much can be attributed to several contributing factors for FICO's being the standard for creditworthiness in this sector. The first among these is the company's unwavering commitment especially accuracy fairness dependability while determining ones credits score. In terms of providing consistent and predictive measures of risk based on consumer information, nothing beats FICO scores since they are grounded on vast researches and scrutiny through users' files.

Moreover, these rating models are reviewed continuously so that changes in consumer behavior can be captured by them as well as changes in regulatory requirements governing lending institutions. This way it stays ahead with respect to emerging trends within the field of loaning hence maintaining confidence with regulators as well as consumers.

Additionally, due to their various product lines such as mortgages auto loans credit cards personal loans among others; these rankings have been absorbed into financial sectors' infrastructures being used as standard measures for assessing risks involved with lending money. Consequently, FICO Scores have turned into a synonymous term representing whether you are able to get loans or not and even your loan interest rates, loan insurance premiums, and rental applications among other things.

What is Vantage Score?

The three biggest credit reporting agencies (TransUnion, Experian, and Equifax) created a credit scoring model called Vantage Score. However, in contrast to the FICO score that was designed by Fair Isaac Corporation, the Vantage Score brings out new ideas on credit valuation.

Other models of credit score like the Vantage Score are based on assessing a variety of indicators. Credit history is one of the factors taken into account during these processes thus payment history, age of your accounts in collection and any others will be thoroughly vetted through computations by this credit scoring model. Its output ranges from 300 to 850, with higher numbers meaning less riskiness associated with credits issued. In deciding whether to grant a loan or not, the Vantage Score is crucial. When you apply for a mortgage loan and other loans such as auto loan, personal loan or even applying for a credit card lender check your credit score first before deciding to give you money or not.

And there you have it - the full 360-degree view of the credit landscape. We have covered the fundamentals from the purpose of credit reporting to the intricate calculation of scores. You now understand the immense power credit wields over your financial life along with the key laws enacted to protect consumer rights.

Armed with this knowledge, you can approach credit consciously instead of letting an arbitrary 3-digit number control your fate. You have both the understanding of how to build stellar credit responsibly AND recourse to set things right if errors outside your control cause setbacks.

The road to good credit requires diligence - but now you have a detailed map of the territory ahead. With vision, perseverance, and the will to overcome obstacles, you can establish robust credit that unlocks life's dreams. It may not be easy, but success is assuredly within reach thanks to newfound clarity on where you stand and how far you have to go.

CHAPTER 2.
UNDERSTANDING CREDIT SCORES

Your credit score—that mysterious three-digit number that holds so much power over your financial life. Yet few truly understand what goes into a credit score and how to improve it. This chapter will demystify credit scores, empowering you to take control and leverage your score to access better rates and opportunities.

We will explore what factors shape your credit score, from payment history to credit utilization to mix of credit. You will learn best practices to build up a strong score over time. We will also bust myths about quick-fix solutions while highlighting legitimate techniques to give your score a boost.

With knowledge comes power. This chapter will equip you to understand the inner workings of credit scoring models, spot inaccuracies on your reports, and constructively build up your profile. Whether applying for a mortgage, auto loan or credit card, you will learn how to put your best score forward at the right times. We will also provide tips to protect your score from unnecessary hits.

Armed with the tools and knowledge from this chapter, you will have the keys to drive your credit score higher and reap rewards from better credit. No longer will your score be a mystery—you will be empowered to make it work for you over the long run. Let us get started uncovering the facts so you can build credit effectively.

Credit Score and its Importance

Your credit score is like a financial grade, condensed into a three-digit number. It is not just a numerical label; it is a crucial measure of your creditworthiness, determining how likely you are to repay borrowed money. This magic number ranges from 300 to 850, with higher scores reflecting better financial health. It gives potential lenders a picture of how likely you are to repay a loan on time. Your credit score is one of the most important factors lenders use to decide whether to give you credit and what interest rates to charge you.

Why is it important? Well, it is the gateway to financial opportunities. When you apply for a loan, a credit card, or a mortgage, lenders peek at your credit score to assess the risk of lending you money. A higher score often leads to better interest rates and more favorable terms, while a lower score might make lenders a bit more cautious.

Let's break it down:

- 300-579: Poor. Lenders might see you as a risky bet.
- 580-669: Fair. You are on the radar, but rates might not be the best.
- 670-739: Good. You are a solid borrower.
- 740-799: Very Good. Lenders are likely rolling out the red carpet.
- 800-850: Excellent. You are the financial VIP, enjoying the best deals.

It opens doors to favorable interest rates, higher credit limits, and smoother financial transactions. Understanding its importance is the first step to mastering the art of financial navigation.

Maintaining a high credit score has many benefits:

- Lower interest rates on loans and credit cards. The higher your credit score, the lower the interest rate a lender is likely to offer you. Thus, saving you significant money, especially on large loans like mortgages and auto loans. For example, someone with a FICO score of 750+ could receive a 30-year fixed mortgage with an Annual Percentage Rate (APR) lower than someone with a FICO score under 670. Saving the person thousands of dollars over the course of the mortgage.

- Improved approval odds and terms. Lender's view borrowers with higher scores as lower risk. You are more likely to get approved for credit and often with better terms like higher credit limits or lower security deposit requirements.

- Increased ability to rent property. Many landlords check credit reports and scores before renting out units. A high score improves your chances of approval and securing desirable rental properties.

- Lower insurance premiums. Auto and home insurers often use credit-based insurance scores to set premiums. Maintaining a high score can mean significant savings on insurance costs over time.

Your credit score is not just important when you are borrowing money; it can also impact other aspects of your life. Landlords may check your credit score before renting you an apartment, and employers may consider it as part of the hiring process. So, maintaining a good credit score is not just about financial flexibility; it is about opening doors to opportunities in various aspects of your life.

How your credit score is calculated

Your credit score is calculated based on the information in your credit report. The most used credit scoring model is the FICO score, which ranges from 300 to 850. Here are the main factors that determine your FICO credit score and their relative importance:

- Payment History (35% of score) Whether you pay your bills on time, including credit cards, retail accounts, utilities, and loans. Delinquent payments, bankruptcies, foreclosures, tax liens, wage garnishments, and judgments negatively impact your score.
- Credit Utilization (30% of score) The ratio between total credit card balances versus total available credit limits across all cards. High utilization exceeding 30% of limits can start to negatively affect your score. Keeping this ratio low is beneficial.

- Credit History Length (15% of score) How long you have had credit accounts opened. Established credit history over many years improves your score. Too many new accounts can negatively affect your score.
- Credit Mix (10% of score) Having different types of credit - mortgage loans, installment loans, credit cards, etc. A healthy mix helps your score rather than only having credit cards.
- New Credit (10% of score) Opening many new credit accounts in a short period can negatively impact your score. However, judicious use of new credit can help strengthen your mix of accounts.

Checks your credit report regularly and focus on the above categories to maintain or improve your credit score over time. Pay all bills on time, keep balances low, allow credit history to lengthen, and be prudent with new credit applications.

Three Major Credit Bureaus

Alright, let's meet the credit gatekeepers – Equifax, Experian, and TransUnion. Think of them as the guardians of your financial reputation. They collect info on your credit behavior and turn it into a report that lenders use to decide if You are a financial hotshot or not.

- **Equifax:**
  Meet the veteran in the game, founded way back in 1899. Equifax is like the wise old owl of credit bureaus. It juggles credit reports for a whopping 820 million individuals and 91 million businesses worldwide. And guess what? They are the maestros behind FICO and Vantage credit scores, using the data they have gathered over the years. If you want a free annual checkup on your credit or need a bodyguard against identity theft, Equifax has your back.

- **Experian:**
  This one is a bit of a globetrotter. Founded in 1996, Experian has its headquarters in Dublin, Ireland. It is like the data explorer, collecting and maintaining credit info on over 1.3 billion consumers

and businesses around the world. Operating Experian CreditWorks, it is your buddy for credit monitoring and identity theft resolution services. And the best part? You can grab your credit report for free through their website – a handy tool for keeping tabs on your financial health.

- **TransUnion:**
  The relative newbie, in business since 1968 – TransUnion has been rocking the credit scene for over 50 years. They're like the innovators, bringing cool products to the table. With over 1 billion credit files globally, they have got some serious data chops. Ever heard of TrueIdentity identity theft protection or the CreditView dashboard? Yep, that is TransUnion's handiwork. If you are willing to shell out a few bucks, they offer monthly updated credit reports and scores, keeping you in the know.

So, there you have it – Equifax, Experian, and TransUnion, your financial guardians. Each has its own flavor, and knowing their backstory helps you navigate the credit landscape like a pro. It is like having a trio of advisors giving you the inside scoop on your financial game plan. Keep them in mind as you make your financial moves, and you'll be one step closer to acing the credit game.

Tips to improve your credit card usage and payment history

Here are some straightforward tips to improve how you use credit cards and your payment history:

- **Pay Your Balance In Full Each Month**
  The best practice is to pay off your entire credit card balance by the due date each month. This avoids interest charges and demonstrates responsible usage. Even if you cannot pay in full, always make at least the minimum payment on time.

- **Keep Your Credit Utilization Low**
  Do not max out your credit cards. Experts recommend keeping your balances below 30% of your total credit limit across all cards. The lower the better for your credit score.

- **Set Payment Reminders**
  Mark your monthly payment due dates on your calendar and set payment alerts/reminders to avoid ever missing payments. Setting up autopay is an easy option that provides additional assurance payments happen on time.

- **Avoid Closing Old Credit Card Accounts**
  Do not close your oldest credit cards as longer open account history helps your credit score. Use older cards periodically to keep them active.

- **Review Statements Regularly**
  Carefully review charges to quickly catch any unauthorized transactions or fraudulent activity. Promptly contacting your issuer regarding disputes also limits potential problems.

- **Check Your Credit Report**
  Check your credit report a few times a year to catch any reporting errors early that could unjustly impact your score or lead to issues with identity theft.

Sticking to these simple habits will lead to improved credit through a proven track record of on-time payments, low balances, and financial responsibility. A strong payment history and credit score saves substantially on loan interest over time.

Understanding Credit Repair

Credit repair is the process of rectifying inaccuracies, incompleteness, or unverifiable information on your credit report. You may have encountered enticing advertisements promising the removal of various negative items like foreclosures, bankruptcies, or tax liens. While it is not as effortless as these ads often claim, credit repair can significantly enhance poor credit scores.

The essence of credit repair lies in methodically challenging incorrect, erroneous, or disputable entries on your credit report. This guide aims to demystify the credit repair process by presenting it in simple, actionable steps.

The roots of credit repair trace back to the Fair Credit Reporting Act of 1971. This pivotal legislation bestowed upon ordinary consumers, such as ourselves, essential rights to ensure the accuracy of our credit reports. If we identify any inaccuracies, we possess the authority to dispute and potentially remove or rectify them.

The exact language in the Act reads:

"If the completeness or accuracy of any item of information contained in a consumer's file at a consumer reporting agency is disputed by the consumer and the consumer notifies the agency directly of such dispute, the agency shall reinvestigate, free of charge, and record the current status of the disputed information, or delete the item from the file in accordance with paragraph (5), before the end of the 30-day period beginning on the date on which the agency receives the notice of the dispute from the consumer."

Over the past few decades, the Fair Credit Reporting Act (FCRA) has undergone numerous updates and amendments, expanding our rights as consumers. A significant addition was made in 2003 with the introduction of the Fair and Accurate Credit Transaction Act (FACTA), which granted us the ability to access our credit reports for free each year through annualcreditreport.com. Prior to this change, free reports were only available if credit had been denied. This development was monumental as it empowered individuals to take proactive steps in credit repair by obtaining their credit reports, an essential first step in the process.

Once we obtain our credit reports, we can meticulously examine them for inaccuracies and discrepancies. Any items that are challenged or disputed prompt creditors to either validate their accuracy or remove them from our reports. It is crucial to note that credit bureaus, collection agencies, and original creditors are legally obligated to adhere to these dispute resolutions under the FCRA.

Understanding the FCRA and our rights as consumers to challenge information on our credit reports forms the cornerstone of the credit repair process. In this guide, readers will gain insights into the inner workings of the credit bureau system and learn how to leverage complex systems such as OCR and e-OSCAR to their advantage. Additionally, advanced dispute tactics will be explored to expedite the credit repair process.

While the FCRA lays the foundation for credit repair, employing advanced dispute methods can further accelerate progress towards achieving excellent credit. Armed with these tools and knowledge, individuals can take control of their financial well-being and secure the credit they deserve.

Factors affecting your credit score

Absolutely! Let's dive deeper into the factors that sway your credit score, all while keeping things light, conversational, and easy to digest.

1. Payment History:

Alright, let us kick things off with payment history – the bread and butter of your credit score. It is like keeping a clean slate with your financial obligations. Paying your bills on time is crucial here. Think of it as honoring your promises to pay back what you owe, and doing so consistently paints you as a reliable borrower in the eyes of lenders. Slip-ups like late payments can send your score south faster than a penguin on an ice slide.

2. Credit Utilization Ratio:

Now, onto the credit utilization ratio – it is like the portion control of the credit world. You want to show lenders you can handle credit responsibly without going overboard. Aim to keep your credit card balances below 30% of your available credit. Think of it as not maxing out your credit cards like they're going out of style. Keeping things in check here signals that you are not living on the financial edge and can manage your credit responsibly.

3. Length of Credit History:

Ah, the length of credit history – it is like the seasoned veteran of your credit score. The longer it is been around, the more clout it carries. Lenders like to see a track record of responsible borrowing over time. It is like proving you have been playing the credit game for a while and know the ropes. So even if you are just dipping your toes into the credit pool, remember that time is your friend – every month you add to your credit history beefs up your financial street cred.

4. Types of Credit Used:

Now, let us talk about the types of credit you are juggling. It is like having a diverse portfolio of financial instruments. Lenders want to see that you can handle different types of credit – from credit cards to loans – with finesse. It is like showing them you are not a one-trick pony when it comes to managing your financial obligations. So mix it up a bit and show off your versatility.

5. New Credit and Credit Inquiries:

Finally, we have got new credit and credit inquiries. It is like the temptation of shiny new toys in the credit world. While it is exciting to open new credit accounts, doing so too often can raise eyebrows among lenders. It is like signaling to them that you might be in over your head financially. Plus, each time a lender peeks at your credit report (a.k.a. a credit inquiry), it can put a little dent in your score. So, think twice before diving headfirst into a flurry of new credit applications.

And there you have it – the lowdown on the factors that sway your credit score. Understanding how each piece of the puzzle fits together can help you navigate the world of credit with confidence and finesse. So, keep these factors in mind as you chart your financial course, and remember – I'm here to help steer you in the right direction if you ever need a guiding hand!

Are You in Need of Credit repair?

Credit stands as a cornerstone of financial stability, wielding considerable influence over various aspects of our economic lives. From mortgage approvals to rental agreements, from car loans to credit card applications, the health of our credit profiles determines the terms and opportunities available to us. Even utilities, insurance premiums, and job prospects increasingly hinge on creditworthiness.

Building and maintaining good credit is not just about financial transactions—it is about securing peace of mind and unlocking a higher quality of life. With solid credit, you can make purchases without anxiety, avoid hefty security deposits, and pursue career advancements unimpeded by credit-related obstacles.

The toolkit I offer is your pathway to the exceptional credit you deserve and the fulfilling lifestyle it enables.

Understanding the Credit Landscape

Given the pivotal role credit plays, one might assume rigorous oversight ensures the accuracy and fairness of credit reports. Regrettably, this is not the case—no one but you has a vested interest in ensuring your credit report accurately reflects your financial standing.

It is incumbent upon you to regularly scrutinize your credit reports. With error rates in credit reporting nearing a staggering 80%, any inaccuracies could jeopardize your financial well-being and peace of mind.

In this chapter, we shed light on the unsung hero of credit scores – the age of your credit history. Remember, it is not just about the numbers; it is about the story you are telling through your financial journey.

As you embark on this credit score adventure, always keep in mind that your financial life is a narrative you are crafting. The decisions you make today shape the chapters of tomorrow. Boosting the age of your credit history is like adding a timeless chapter, showcasing your financial responsibility and resilience.

So, pat yourself on the back for leveling up your credit score wisdom. In the next chapter, we will tackle the intricacies of understanding your credit report.

CHAPTER 3: UNDERSTANDING YOUR CREDIT REPORT

Welcome to the heart of your financial story – your credit report. In this chapter, we will embark on a journey through the intricacies of this essential document. We will decode the sections, understand their significance, and equip you with the knowledge to ensure your financial narrative is accurate and compelling. Your credit report is something of an information free-for-all between you and lending institutions - kind of like a journal detailing your financial highs, lows and everything in between over time. As intimidating as that may seem, learning exactly what goes into this powerful record gives you an advantage when disputes arise.

Your credit report is like a financial diary, documenting your credit history. It consists of several key sections, including personal information, account history, inquiries, and more. Each section plays a crucial role in painting the full picture of your financial health.

Overview of Information on a credit report:

Personal Information: you will find basic identification content like your full name (including any aliases or name variations you have used to obtain credit), current and previous addresses for the last couple of years, your date of birth, and the last 4-5 digits of your SSN. This section enables lenders to definitively match you to your credit history without mixing files up with borrowers of similar names.

Some reports may also list current or former employers along with your income to provide additional context around your financial situation. Misinformation like inaccurate former addresses or employers must be disputed as it raises questions on if negative items belong to you or not when lending decisions are being made.

Account History

It shows where all credit-related activities are chronicled for potential lenders to review. This comprehensive section details your current and past credit accounts like credit cards, retail cards, auto loans, mortgages, student loans and personal lines of credit. Information provided includes:

- The type of account (credit card, auto loan etc.)
- The date the account was opened
- The account status (open, paid/closed, defaulted)
- The date of last activity if closed
- The amount of credit extended (credit limit, original loan amount, highest balance)
- The current balance still owed
- Minimum monthly payment amounts
- Your payment history and delinquency details

Inquiries

The inquiries section of your credit report shows hard credit account inquiries made when lenders check your history because you applied for credit. These include credit cards, personal loans, mortgages, auto financing, and the like.

Hard inquiries can lower scores temporarily when you have a lot in a short span, implying higher risk since you seem credit-hungry. However, their impact fades over about a year. Too many in quick succession may make lenders skittish.

Soft inquiries also appear but do not affect your scores at all. Soft checks only show you what pre-qualified offers lenders will extend but involve no commitment. Pre-approvals for financing offers also show here but are not counted against your rating.

Account Summary:

The account summary section in your credit report provides a comprehensive overview of your financial standing. It includes information on the number of open and closed accounts, types of accounts (such as revolving and installment), real estate holdings, outstanding debts, collections, and more. It is crucial to carefully review each aspect. Verify if the balances on your accounts are accurate, both for closed and current accounts. Additionally, comparing information across different credit bureau reports is essential. Discrepancies are common, so investigate them thoroughly. Expect variations in reported data, including total account numbers, debt amounts, and individual account balances and payments. Pay particular attention to the Derogatory section, focusing on inquiries, public records, collections, and past delinquencies. Ideally, this section should reflect zeros post-dispute and serves as a gauge for monitoring your credit progress.

Public Records:

The public records section divulges details regarding bankruptcies, judgments, tax liens, and other legal matters. This segment significantly impacts your credit report and requires immediate attention. Scrutinize each entry meticulously, noting record types, court details, filing dates, and relevant information for dispute purposes. It is common for bankruptcies to be inaccurately reported, with a lasting impact of up to 10 years. Unpaid judgments and tax liens can linger on your report for a decade or more, or indefinitely, respectively. Given their severity, prioritize addressing issues within the public records section. Specialized dispute strategies may be necessary for these challenging accounts.

Additional Details:

Credit monitoring services offer various specialized sections in credit reports, each providing unique insights. Platforms like Credit Check

Total furnish specific details such as factors influencing credit scores, comprehensive credit pattern analyses, and in-depth examinations of discrepancies. Take advantage of these additional resources to glean valuable information beyond the standard report. Embrace these supplementary features, as they constitute part of the service You are investing in, enhancing your overall understanding of your credit profile.

How to Obtain Your Credit Reports from the Three Bureaus

All right, let's cut through the confusion and get you your credit reports – it is like checking your financial health report card. Here's the easy-peasy guide:

Before disputes can even commence, assessing your standing requires getting your hands on your current credit reports from each bureau. Let us discuss the range of options to obtain the invaluable intel needed to launch a credit repair crusade.

AnnualCreditReport.com – Your Gateway to Free Yearly Reports

The government-authorized website AnnualCreditReport.com allows everyone to access free credit reports from Experian, Equifax, and Transunion once every 12 months. This covers you to check all three bureaus for free once annually.

Spreading out requests is ideal for consistent monitoring. Checking one agency every four months yields a report from each bureau three times annually without any payment. Do not sleep on this essential option for catching issues early!

Step-by-step Guide:

- Visit AnnualCreditReport.com: This is your golden ticket to free credit reports. It is the one-stop shop where you can grab reports from Equifax, Experian, and TransUnion.

- Verify Your Identity: It is like a digital handshake. They might ask you questions about your past addresses, loans, or that time you had a pet rock. It is just to make sure it is really you.
- Choose Your Reports: You have three amigos – Equifax, Experian, and TransUnion. You can get them all at once or stagger them throughout the year. It is like spreading out the joy of unwrapping presents.

Identifying Errors and Issues in Your Reports

It is like checking your reflection in the mirror – you want it to be spot on. Here's how to spot and fix any hiccups in your financial tale.

Think of your credit report as your financial report card. Lenders, landlords, and sometimes even potential employers' peek. You want it to be as clear as possible because it can influence whether you get that loan, an apartment, or even a job.

Different Types of Errors:

Now, let us get into the nitty-gritty. Errors can range from simple mistakes to signs of identity theft. Here are a few things to keep an eye on:

- Incorrect Personal Information: Check your name, address, and employment details. If anything looks off, it is time to raise an eyebrow. For instance, if the report says you worked at a pizza joint, but you have been in IT for the last five years, that is a red flag.
- Account Discrepancies: Look at your credit card, loan, and mortgage details. Ensure the balances, payment history, and credit limits align with your memory. If there is a card you closed ages ago but it is still showing active, that is something to fix.
- Fraudulent Activity: Keep an eye out for accounts you do not recognize. If there's a credit card or loan you never signed up

for, someone might be using your financial identity. Time to act fast.

What to Do When You Spot an Error:

- Dispute Inaccuracies: If you find a mistake, do not panic. You have the right to dispute it. Contact the credit bureau, explain the error, and provide any supporting documents.
- Stay Persistent: Resolving errors can take some time. Be patient and stay persistent. Check back to ensure corrections are made.
- Stay Informed: Regularly check your credit report. Catching errors early is like fixing a leaky roof before it becomes a waterfall in your living room.

Your credit report is your financial fingerprint. It should tell your story, not someone else's. Regular check-ups ensure accuracy and help you catch any hiccups before they turn into headaches. So, grab that financial magnifying glass and make sure your credit report is a true reflection of your journey.

Applying for Credit / Inquiries

Alright, let's talk about applying for credit and the impact it has on your credit report – especially those pesky inquiries. When you are thinking about getting a new credit card or a loan, it is like dipping your toe into the credit pool. But before you dive in, it is essential to understand how it all works.

First up, there are two types of inquiries: soft pulls and hard pulls.

- **Soft Pulls:** These are like peeking at your own report. You might do this when checking your credit score or getting a pre-approved offer in the mail. They do not affect your credit score, so feel free to take a look whenever you want.
- **Hard Pulls:** Now, these are the ones tied to actual credit applications – like when you apply for a credit card or a loan.

These inquiries do impact your credit score, albeit temporarily. Too many hard pulls in a short period can make lenders a little wary, so it is best to space out your credit applications.

You know how some things have an expiration date? Well, inquiries on your credit report are no different.

How Long Do They Stick Around? Typically, inquiries stay on your report for about two years. After that, they vanish into the credit report abyss. But do not worry, their impact fades over time, so it is not a permanent stain on your financial record. Applying for credit is like dipping your toes into the credit pool – it can be refreshing if you do it right. Just remember to be mindful of how often you are making a splash with those credit applications. Soft pulls are harmless, but keep an eye on those hard pulls and space them out to avoid any ripples in your credit score pond.

- **Bankruptcies:** Picture this as a financial reset button. When someone faces overwhelming debts and can't climb out, they might file for bankruptcy. It is a tough decision, but it wipes the slate clean, giving them a chance to start anew. However, it is a heavyweight on a credit report and can stick around for seven to ten years.
- **Charge-offs:** When a lender gives up on getting you to repay a debt, it is called a charge-off. It is like admitting defeat on their end. While it does not mean You are off the hook for the debt, it signals a significant hit to your credit score.
- **Late Payments:** Life gets hectic, and sometimes bills slip through the cracks. Late payments are common, but they come with consequences. A single late payment can ding your credit, and the later payments you accumulate, the more the impact grows.
- **Collections:** If you have ignored a debt long enough, it might end up in collections. This is when a third-party agency steps in to try to collect what's owed. It is not a guest appearance you want in your credit report, as it can significantly lower your score.

- **Foreclosures:** A home foreclosure happens when you can't keep up with your mortgage payments, and the lender takes possession of your property. It is a serious hit to your credit and can affect your ability to get a new mortgage for several years.
- **Public Records:** This is the grand stage where legal matters unfold. Think tax liens, judgments, or bankruptcies. These are matters of public record that can cast a shadow on your creditworthiness.

Negative entries on your credit report are like plot twists – they add drama to the story. But remember, they do not define your financial narrative forever. Understanding their impact and differentiating between them is the first step to overcoming these hurdles

Congratulations! You have just decoded the elements of your credit report. Armed with this knowledge, you have the power to ensure its accuracy and use it as a tool for your financial success. In the next chapter, we will navigate the terrain of dealing with issues on your credit report – a crucial step in crafting a financial narrative that truly reflects you. Ready for the next chapter?

CHAPTER 4: DEALING WITH ISSUES

Ever felt the sting of a late payment or the looming shadow of a collection notice? Fear not, because in this chapter, we are arming you with practical strategies. Picture this as your credit rescue toolkit, complete with communication tips, negotiation hacks, and real-life examples of individuals who turned their credit stories around.

So, fasten your financial seatbelt, because we are diving into the strategies for handling late payments, collections, and more. By the end of this chapter, you will be equipped with the skills to navigate the twists and turns of credit challenges. Ready to embark on this credit repair adventure? Let us get started!

Practical tips for addressing late payments

- Addressing Late Payments: Late payments happen to the best of us. Maybe you had a hectic month, or the due date slipped your mind. The key here is communication. Reach out to your creditor as soon as you realize there is an issue. Explain the situation and see if they are willing to work with you.
- Handling Collections: Seeing an account in collections can be stressful, but it is not the end of the road. First, validate the debt – make sure it is accurate. If it is, consider negotiating with the collection agency. They might be open to settling the debt for less than the full amount or setting up a manageable payment plan.

Communication is your secret weapon. Whether you are dealing with late payments or collections, taking the initiative to talk to your creditors or collection agencies can make a world of difference.

How to Handle Erroneous Entries and Fraud

Having errors or fraudulent activity on your credit report can significantly lower your credit score and make it harder to get approved for loans, mortgages, credit cards, and other financial products. It is important to regularly check your credit report from the three major credit bureaus - Experian, TransUnion, and Equifax to catch any inaccuracies early on.

Check Credit Reports Regularly

The first step is to obtain free copies of your credit reports from annualcreditreport.com once every year from each of the three bureaus. Carefully review the entries on all accounts like loans, credit cards, collections etc. Cross check facts like account numbers, payment history, outstanding balances, employment history among others. Any discrepancies need to be flagged.

Common Errors to Look Out For:

- ☐ Accounts that do not belong to you
- ☐ Incorrect personal information
- ☐ Closed accounts still listed as open
- ☐ Wrong credit limits or balances
- ☐ Multiple listings of debt
- ☐ Late payments incorrectly listed

Signs of Possible Fraud:

- ☐ New credit cards/loan accounts opened without your knowledge
- ☐ Inquiries from lenders that you do not recognize
- ☐ Addresses listed that you never lived at

How to Dispute Errors or Fraud

If you notice mistakes or fraudulent activity, you should dispute the information by contacting both the credit bureau and your lenders/banks. Inform them in writing of what the issue is along with copies of any evidence like account numbers/payment receipts. Ask for an investigative dispute case to be opened. Under the Fair Credit Reporting Act, they are mandated to investigate and remove unverifiable, inaccurate, or fraudulent entries. Bank fraud departments also look into disputed accounts.

Monitoring your credit report vigilantly is key to maintaining a healthy credit score. Ensure that you catch any erroneous/fraudulent entries early before they cascade into bigger issues. Understand the rules of credit bureaus on fraud disputes and leverage them fully. Being persistent and having documentary evidence is crucial till resolution.

Writing Effective Dispute Letters to Bureaus

Alright, time to put pen to paper – or fingers to keyboard – and craft a dispute letter that gets results. Writing an effective dispute letter to credit bureaus might feel a bit like a game of chess, but with the right moves, you can checkmate those errors. Let's break it down.

Crafting Your Defense:

- **Step 1: Your Information**
  Start with your basic details. It is like saying, "Hey, this is me, and I need your attention." Be clear about your full name, address, and the specific item You are disputing.

- **Step 2: The Error Unveiling**
  Next, unveil the error like a detective presenting evidence. Specify the inaccurate information, whether it is a mysterious account you never opened or an incorrect payment record.

- **Step 3: The Why Behind Your Dispute**
  Explain why you are disputing the item. Maybe it is a case of mistaken identity, or perhaps you have paid off a debt that still shows as outstanding. Lay out the facts and make it clear why this information is inaccurate.

- **Step 4: The Proof is in the Pudding**
  If you have any supporting documents – receipts, letters, or anything that backs your case – include them. It is like attaching exhibits to your argument. The more evidence, the stronger your case.

- **Step 5: The Request for Action**
  Politely but firmly ask the credit bureau to investigate and correct the error. This is your call to action – the moment you say, "I have presented my case, now it is your turn to make it right."

<u>Communication with Credit Bureaus:</u>

Now, let's talk tone. Be firm, but there is no need for a legal thriller. Keep it clear, concise, and to the point. Avoid unnecessary jargon; You are having a conversation, not writing a legal brief.

Ensuring Comprehensive Dispute Letters

Begin each dispute letter with accurate details, including your full name, social security number, and current address. The credit bureaus necessitate this information to authenticate your identity before processing any dispute. Your social security number serves as the primary link between your dispute and credit report, so it is crucial to provide it clearly.

Additionally, enclose supporting documentation to validate your identity, such as your Driver's License and Social Security Card. Failure to include these may result in the dismissal of your disputes. If you lack a driver's license or Social Security card, alternative forms of identification like a passport or state ID can suffice. Including documents like pay stubs or W2 forms, displaying both your name and social security number, can also serve this purpose.

Remember, omitting a picture ID or document verifying your social security number will hinder the investigation of your disputes. Ensure these are enclosed with each correspondence.

Furthermore, specify the account name and number in your letter along with the reason for dispute. Some creditors report distinct account numbers to each bureau, so accuracy is paramount. Verify that the correct account number for the respective bureau is included in your dispute letter.

Awaiting and Reviewing Results

Anticipate observing outcomes within 30-45 days, although variations may occur. The Fair and Accurate Credit Transaction Act mandates creditors to respond within 30 days from the date the dispute is entered into e-OSCAR by the credit bureaus.

Allow for the mailing of disputes to the credit bureau and for the initiation of the dispute process, which collectively justify the 40-45 days waiting period. Request in your dispute letter that the bureau responds via mail, as mandated by law. Subsequently, the credit bureaus will dispatch copies of your credit reports by mail, often in oversized envelopes with P.O. Box return addresses.

Typically, the results will be prominent on the first page of the received reports.

Trans Union's reports boast a user-friendly format, presenting results upfront on the initial page in a neatly organized list. Each entry includes the account name, number, and the outcome of the dispute. The desired outcome is typically "DELETED," although alternatives such as "VERIFIED" or "NO CHANGE" may appear. Occasionally, you might encounter "NEW INFORMATION BELOW," indicating a minor adjustment to the reported data rather than the removal of the negative item. These modifications could involve alterations to the date of last activity, outstanding balance, or other relevant factors prompting the dispute. Trans Union provides detailed account information, granting access to your online credit report for thorough examination. This direct access offers valuable insight into precisely what Trans Union reports about your credit status, ensuring accuracy beyond what credit monitoring services may provide. Review your reports diligently and record the results as instructed in the subsequent Track Results section of this guide.

Experian's reports may present results on either the first or second page, accompanied by a summary list outlining account name, numbers, and statuses. Desired outcomes include "Deleted," while "Remains" signifies the worst-case scenario, indicating the item's persistence on the report without alteration. "Updated" denotes a modification to the item without its removal. If the dispute concerns ownership, a "Verified" status confirms the item's validity. "Reviewed" suggests the need for personal inspection of the report to discern whether a deletion or update occurred. Experian furnishes additional account details, including creditor information and filing dates, facilitating a comprehensive understanding of the report.

Equifax reports lack a concise summary section, necessitating a thorough review of individual account details to identify changes. Typically, updated and deleted accounts are displayed within the first two pages under headings like "The Results of Our Investigation" and "Collection Agency." These sections provide a succinct account of dispute outcomes, listing creditor names, account numbers, and a brief statement summarizing the results. Desired outcomes mirror those of other credit bureaus, with a preference for deletions. Equifax specifies updates in the summary description, guiding a meticulous review to highlight remaining negative accounts. Credit bureau reports offer abundant additional details absent from monitoring reports, each potentially warranting further dispute consideration.

Understanding certain key indicators on your credit report is crucial for managing your financial health effectively. Among these are the "Last Reported" date provided by Experian, the "Date Paid" information from Trans Union, and the "Date of 1st Delinquency" recorded by Equifax. These indicators signify significant moments in your financial history, such as the last activity or payment made on an account.

The importance of these dates lies in their influence on how long negative entries remain on your credit report. Typically, derogatory accounts persist for seven years from the date of the initial delinquency, marking the period when you first fell behind on payments without subsequently bringing the account up to date. It is crucial to take note of this date as it dictates the duration of the negative impact on your report.

However, certain financial setbacks, such as bankruptcies, unpaid judgments, and tax liens, can linger on your report for a decade or more. This underscores the significance of considering the implications before addressing older accounts or collections, especially since merely paying off a debt may not lead to its removal from your report.

In some cases, creditors or collection agencies may agree to delete negative items from your report in exchange for payment, a practice known as "Pay-to-Delete." Yet, it is important to note that this is not always a feasible outcome. More often, they may offer to update or correct your report to reflect a zero balance or settled status upon payment. However, these adjustments may have limited impact on improving your credit scores, as the presence of a collection account itself carries negative weight.

Your credit score essentially serves as a predictive tool, assessing the likelihood of you becoming severely delinquent on an account within the next two years. Once an account has entered collections, it signals a heightened risk of future delinquency, regardless of whether you settle the debt thereafter. In essence, paying off a collection does not mitigate the underlying risk associated with past delinquency.

This understanding underscores why paying off collections may offer minimal benefit to your credit standing. Consequently, if you opt to address a collection, settling the debt rather than paying it in full is often recommended. Ultimately, whether settled or paid in full, a collection entry maintains its negative impact on your credit report.

DO IT AGAIN!

Upon completing your review, diligently record the outcomes in your Dispute Log. Thoroughly scrutinize your reports to identify lingering negative items. Early disputes often yield significant removals as they help pinpoint creditors with sufficient data to report on your profile.

It is not uncommon for creditors to maintain inadequate records or to discard them when transferring accounts to collections. Hence, a simple dispute, for any reason, can lead to the removal of numerous such accounts.

Expect to encounter creditors who either verify or update the account information. These are the entities you'll need to persistently dispute with to expunge the items.

Once your log is updated with the persisting negative creditors, follow the steps to send out another batch of disputes to the credit bureaus.

REMEMBER, each dispute should cite a different reason, supported by appropriate documentation or a request for the bureau's investigation method. Avoid filing repetitive disputes without substantiation to prevent them from being deemed frivolous.

Consistently dispute with the credit bureaus every month. After a couple of rounds, you'll start identifying your primary "problem creditors," typically those reporting your most recent data. While eliminating these accounts might demand more effort, you'll still achieve success in having many of them erased.

Following the initial rounds of disputes, consider implementing some of the Advanced Dispute strategies outlined later in this guide. Simultaneous disputes with both the credit bureau and original creditors tend to yield better results in removing recent and more detrimental accounts.

Begin with credit bureau disputes to identify the most challenging creditors. On average, these disputes should result in the deletion of 40-60% of your total negatives.

Remember to review your results upon receiving responses from the credit bureaus, update your log, and promptly initiate another round of disputes. You do not need to wait for responses from all bureaus; if one responds first, proceed with the next dispute without delay.

Be aware that some credit bureaus may delay or omit sending back reports. If you haven't received results within 40 days, check your credit monitoring account for updates. Often, the bureaus conduct investigations without mailing results. In such cases, utilize your updated credit report from the monitoring service to track outcomes, update your Dispute Log, and send out subsequent disputes for remaining negative accounts

Sample Dispute Letter:

Your Name
Your Address
City, State, ZIP Code
Date
Credit Bureau's Name
Credit Bureau's Address
City, State, ZIP Code

Subject: Dispute of Inaccurate Information on My Credit Report

Dear [Credit Bureau's Name],

I hope this letter finds you well. My name is [Your Full Name], and I am writing to dispute an item on my credit report.

I recently reviewed my credit report and noticed an error regarding [Specify the inaccuracy - e.g., an account I never opened / an incorrect payment record]. After careful examination, I believe this information is inaccurate, and I would like to request an investigation into the matter.

Details of the error: [Specify the details of the error, including the account name, account number, and any other relevant information].

Explanation of the dispute: [Clearly explain why you are disputing the item, providing any supporting details].

Supporting documentation: [Attach any supporting documents you have, such as receipts, letters, or any evidence that strengthens your case].

I kindly request that you investigate this matter and correct the inaccuracies on my credit report. Your prompt attention to this issue is greatly appreciated.

Thank you for your time and assistance in resolving this matter. I look forward to a prompt resolution.

Sincerely,

[Your Full Name]

Remember, this is just a template. Tailor it to fit your specific situation, and make sure to send it via certified mail with a return receipt requested to keep track of the communication. Good luck, and may your credit report be error-free!

Credit Bureau Delay Tactics

Credit bureaus often employ tactics to slow down the credit improvement process, a strategy known as "Stall Tactics" within the credit industry. These methods can hinder the dispute process, and it is essential to be aware of them. Let's explore some of the most common ones.

ID Request: A common tactic is for the credit bureau to request identification along with your dispute. Failure to provide identification can be cited as a reason to delay processing your dispute. Therefore, it is crucial to ensure that your IDs are submitted with every dispute you make.

Fraud Allegation: Even if you have submitted your IDs, you might receive a letter from the credit bureau alleging fraud and requesting your IDs again. It is important not to be discouraged by this tactic. Anticipate such responses as part of the credit bureau's strategy. In your Dispute Template Library, I have provided a standard response letter for this situation. This letter asserts that you have already submitted your IDs and reminds the bureau of their reduced timeframe to complete the dispute.

Legal Timeframe: Remember, according to the law, credit bureaus have 30 days to obtain a response from creditors once you initiate a dispute. To determine how much time they have left, check your records for the date you mailed your dispute. Then, subtract the number of days passed from 30 and include this figure in your response letter.

For instance, if the bureau sends you a request for IDs seven days after you mailed the dispute, subtract seven from 30, leaving 23 days. Use the template letter to inform the bureau that they now have 23 days, as mandated by law, to respond to the dispute, reiterating that the excuse of lacking IDs is unacceptable both to you and under legal terms.

By employing this strategy, you can expedite the resolution process and expect results within the typical timeframe.

This is frivolous: This situation may occur infrequently if you adhere to my recommended methods, but it may arise if you attempt to challenge the same account for the same reason. Sometimes, even if your dispute is legitimate, you might receive this response due to tactics employed by credit bureaus, particularly Experian, which has faced legal action over such practices.

Should you receive a response labeling your dispute as frivolous, it is essential to reply using the provided template, asserting that the dispute is indeed valid and that the bureau must adhere to the legally mandated timeframe for investigation. If they persist in labeling your dispute as frivolous, it is prudent to initiate another dispute, citing a different reason.

If subsequent responses continue to dismiss your dispute as frivolous, it becomes necessary to draft another letter reaffirming that you have never disputed the account for the stated reason, reiterating your grounds for dispute, and forwarding it to the bureau. Simultaneously, lodging a complaint with the Fair-Trade Commission for non-compliance with the FCRA can be a strategic step.

By following this course of action, you can challenge the frivolous response effectively and initiate a fresh dispute process.

Negotiating with Your Creditors

All right, let's talk about turning the tables when you find yourself in a tough spot with your creditors. Negotiation is the name of the game, and we've got some practical strategies and communication tips up our sleeves.

<u>Negotiation Approaches:</u>

When you are dealing with financial challenges, a bit of negotiation can go a long way. Whether it is negotiating a lower payoff amount or setting up a reasonable payment plan, finding common ground is key.

It is like finding that sweet spot where both you and your creditor can shake hands and say, "Alright, we can work with this."

Communication Tips

It is not just about what you say; it is about how you say it. We are not talking about fancy lawyer jargon here; we are talking about straightforward, human-to-human conversations.

- Be Honest and Transparent: Lay your cards on the table. If You are facing financial difficulties, be upfront about it. Creditors appreciate honesty, and it opens the door for finding solutions together.
- Propose Realistic Solutions: Do not promise the moon. Be realistic about what you can afford. Whether it isa lump-sum payment or a structured plan, proposing something that fits your budget is the key to a successful negotiation.
- Express Your Willingness to Cooperate: Let them know you are not running away from the situation. Express your commitment to resolving the issue and your willingness to cooperate. It is about showing that you are not avoiding the problem.
- Ask Questions: If there's something you do not understand or if you need more information, do not hesitate to ask. It is your right to have clarity about the terms of any agreement.

Negotiating with creditors does not have to be a daunting task. It is about having open and honest conversations, proposing realistic solutions, and showing that You are committed to finding common ground.

The Dispute Process

Understanding the Levels:

Direct Disputes with Creditors: Imagine you spot an error on your credit report – maybe an account that does not belong to you. The first step is reaching out directly to the creditor. It is like having a one-on-one chat, clearing up any misunderstandings.

Credit Bureaus Involvement: If the direct approach does not cut it, it is time to bring in the big guns – the credit bureaus. They're the referees in this credit game. Submit your dispute to them, and They will investigate, ensuring accuracy in your credit report.

Escalating the Issue: Still not getting the resolution you deserve? It is time to escalate. The Consumer Financial Protection Bureau (CFPB) is like the superhero regulatory body. They step in to make sure things are fair and square.

Time Frames and Limitations:

- Expected Time Frames: Patience is the name of the game. After you have submitted your dispute, give it some time. Credit bureaus typically have 30 days to investigate. It is like waiting for a mystery to unfold – you can't rush it.
- Statutes of Limitations: Now, there is a clock ticking. For some credit report errors, there's a statute of limitations. It is like a timer on the validity of the error. Once that timer buzzes, the error should be wiped off your report.

Navigating the dispute process is a bit like solving a puzzle. You start with the straightforward pieces – direct disputes with creditors. If that does not crack it, you bring in the credit bureaus. And if all else fails, the Consumer Financial Protection Bureau steps up. Remember, patience is your sidekick in this process. It is not a race; it is about getting it right.

Laws on Disputing and the Bureau Responsibility

Okay, let us talk about your rights and the rules of the game when it comes to disputing stuff on your credit report. It is like knowing the playbook to make sure you are treated fairly.

Consumer Rights:

Know the Drill: When you are in dispute mode, it is crucial to understand your rights. The law has got your back. We will delve into the Fair Credit Reporting Act (FCRA) and other relevant regulations that give you the power to challenge inaccuracies.

Fight Fair: We will cover the ground rules – what you can dispute, the timelines for responses, and the steps you can take if things aren't going your way. Spoiler alert: You have got more control than you might think.

Bureau Responsibilities:

Their Job, Your Credit: Credit bureaus are not just passive record keepers. They have responsibilities too. We will explore what they are supposed to do when you throw a dispute their way. Hint: It involves investigating and getting things straight.

Demand Accountability: We will discuss how to hold them accountable for accurate reporting and ensuring they follow the rules laid out by the bigwigs in the regulatory world.

Response Time Requirements

Timelines in Focus:

The Waiting Game: Patience is a virtue, especially when it comes to credit disputes. We will lay out the expected response times from both credit bureaus and creditors. Spoiler alert #2: Sometimes it feels like waiting for a sequel, but your patience will pay off.

Various Games Bureaus Play

Navigating the Challenges:

Hidden Obstacles: Credit bureaus might throw a curveball or two your way. We will discuss the common tactics they use, like verifying information quickly without digging deep. But do not worry – we've got strategies to help you sidestep these obstacles.

Stay Sharp: Being one step ahead is the name of the game. We will help you anticipate and tackle those challenges so you can come out on top of the credit dispute arena.

You have learned your rights, understood the timelines, and even got a sneak peek into the playbook of credit bureaus. Remember, fixing your credit is a journey, not a sprint. In the next chapter, we will switch gears and talk about life after the credit repair hustle – how to keep that credit shining and what steps you can take for a financially robust future. Get ready for the grand finale of our credit saga – it is about to get interesting!

CHAPTER 5: AFTER CREDIT REPAIR

As you turn this page, envision it as opening the door to a world where persistence becomes your secret weapon, patience becomes your armor, and your credit score transforms into a financial superhero. But that is just the beginning. We are about to dive into setting up your financial watchtower, mastering habits that make your credit sing, and knowing precisely when to call in the cavalry

By the end of this chapter, you will not just have information; you will have a personalized blueprint for post-credit-repair success. Picture this as the grand finale of a blockbuster movie where the hero emerges not just triumphant but transformed. Expect insights that stick, strategies that resonate, and a roadmap that leads you to a financial landscape where credit worries become a distant memory.

Persistence and Patience when rebuilding your credit

Rebuilding your credit takes time and dedication. Do not expect your credit score to dramatically improve overnight. Stay persistent in using credit responsibly, and have patience knowing your creditworthiness will gradually increase as positive information remains on your credit reports over time. Remember, past mistakes do not define your financial future if you learn from them. With consistent positive credit behavior, what once seemed like an impossible feat can become reality. Persist a little longer than you want to, because that is when transformation happens. The effort is always worth it.

I know how easy it is to get impatient. You put in all this work - disputing errors, paying down balances, changing bad habits. And what does your credit score do? Barely budges. Infuriating, right?

Here is a truth you need to take to heart: Real change happens slowly. Think of rebuilding credit as a marathon, not a sprint. Drastic spikes and dips will discourage you. But steady, incremental increases will start to snowball, faster than you would expect.

Keep sight on where you are headed, not just the frustrating spot where you stand today. Is your score higher than 3 months ago? 6 months? Any upward step, even small, is noteworthy progress to celebrate.

And if things feel stalled, do not assume the worst. Look closer before losing hope. Perhaps an old collection fell off your report, but you applied for new credit too. The timing affected your score temporarily. But you are still making objectively better financial decisions. So, hang in there.

Here is what I tell my clients who feel like throwing in the towel:

Patience pays exponentially. The effort you are putting in now is a down payment on financial opportunities down the road you likely can't even imagine yet – a future car loan at a prime rate, a dream apartment that just opened up downtown, a refi that saves hundreds per month. This is what awaits when you turn the corner.

But only if you keep at it. Persist a little longer than you want to. That is when transformation happens; when you reap dividends you can't yet see coming.

Stay the course. Be relentless. The best things in life do not come easy; just ask any millionaire. But with perseverance, you will get there and you'll know you earned it.

Setting up Credit Monitoring

Alright, let's dive into the world of credit monitoring – your personal financial watchdog. It is like having a loyal guardian watching over your credit report, ready to alert you to any suspicious activity.

So, what exactly is credit monitoring? Think of it as your financial radar, constantly scanning your credit report for any unusual activity. It is your early warning system, designed to catch identity theft, fraud, or errors on your credit report before they cause major damage.

When you set up credit monitoring, the service keeps a close eye on your credit report from major credit bureaus like Equifax, Experian, and TransUnion. These reports contain detailed information about your credit accounts, payment history, and any inquiries made into your credit file. By regularly reviewing your credit report, you can spot any discrepancies or suspicious activity that could indicate fraud or errors.

But how does credit monitoring alert you to potential problems? Well, most credit monitoring services offer alerts via email, text message, or through their online platform. These alerts notify you of any significant changes to your credit report, such as new accounts opened in your name, late payments reported by creditors, or inquiries into your credit history. Some services even provide real-time monitoring, so You are immediately alerted to any suspicious activity.

Now, you might be wondering: what kind of activity should I be looking out for? Great question! Here are a few red flags to watch for:

- New Accounts: If you did not open a new credit card or loan recently, but notice a new account on your credit report, it could be a sign of identity theft.
- Late Payments: If a creditor reports a late payment on your account, but you know you have been paying on time, it is worth investigating further.
- Inquiries: Keep an eye on any inquiries into your credit report. If you did not authorize a credit check, it could be a sign that someone is trying to open accounts in your name.
- Credit Utilization: High credit card balances relative to your credit limits can negatively impact your credit score. Monitoring your credit can help you keep tabs on your utilization ratio and adjust if needed.

By staying informed about these potential threats to your credit, you can take swift action to protect yourself and minimize the damage. This might involve disputing inaccurate information with the credit bureaus, placing a fraud alert or credit freeze on your credit file, or even filing a police report if you suspect identity theft.

In addition to monitoring for fraud and errors, credit monitoring can also help you track your progress in improving your credit score. By regularly checking your credit report and score, you can see how your financial habits are impacting your credit over time. This can be incredibly empowering, as it allows you to take control of your financial future and make informed decisions about your credit usage.

Now, there are a few different ways you can set up credit monitoring. One option is through your bank or credit card issuer. Many banks offer free credit monitoring services as part of their online banking platforms. This means you can log in to your account and check your credit score and report whenever you like.

Another option is to use third-party credit monitoring services. These companies typically offer more comprehensive monitoring, including alerts for changes to your credit report, suspicious activity, and even identity theft protection. Some popular options include Credit Karma, Identity Guard, and Experian.

But no matter which method you choose, the goal is the same: to stay informed about what's happening with your credit. Monitoring your credit regularly allows you to spot any errors or inaccuracies on your credit report and take action to correct them. It also helps you detect signs of identity theft or fraud early on, minimizing the damage to your finances.

So, how often should you check your credit? Well, that depends on your personal preference and level of concern. Some experts recommend checking your credit report at least once a year, while others suggest monitoring it more frequently, such as quarterly or even monthly.

Ultimately, the more often you check, the better equipped you will be to catch any issues before they spiral out of control.

In addition to monitoring your credit, it is also important to understand what factors can impact your credit score. Payment history, credit utilization, length of credit history, and new credit inquiries all play a role in determining your score. By staying informed about these factors and practicing responsible credit habits, you can help maintain a healthy credit score over time.

In summary, credit monitoring is a powerful tool for protecting your financial health and maintaining a strong credit score. By staying vigilant and proactive about monitoring your credit report, you can catch fraud and errors early on, track your progress in rebuilding your credit, and ultimately achieve your financial goals with confidence.

Maintaining good credit practices

Alright, so you have worked hard to fix up your credit, and now it is time to ensure it stays in tip-top shape. Let us dive deeper into what it takes to maintain good credit practices without getting overwhelmed.

First off, paying your bills on time is non-negotiable. It is not just a suggestion – it is crucial for your credit health. Late payments can have a serious impact on your credit score, dragging it down faster than you can say "oops." Set up reminders, automate payments, whatever it takes to stay on top of those due dates.

Now, let's talk about credit card balances. It is easy to fall into the trap of carrying a balance, especially when life throws unexpected expenses your way. But here's the thing: keeping your credit card balances low is key to keeping your credit score high. Aim to keep your balances below 30% of your credit limit. So, if your credit card has a limit of $1,000, try to keep your balance under $300.

Oh, and speaking of credit cards, let's discuss the temptation of opening new accounts. Sure, that shiny new store card might come with some tempting perks, but every time you apply for a new line of credit, it can ding your credit score a bit. Plus, having too many accounts can make it harder to manage your finances. Stick to the cards you need and resist the urge to sign up for every offer that comes your way.

Another important factor to consider is the length of your credit history. Lenders like to see a long track record of responsible credit use. So, think twice before closing old accounts, even if You are not using them anymore. Keeping those accounts open can actually help boost your credit score in the long run.

Lastly, let's not forget about the importance of monitoring your credit report. You can get a free copy once a year from each of the three major credit bureaus – Equifax, Experian, and TransUnion. Take the time to review your report carefully, looking for any errors or discrepancies. If you spot something fishy, do not hesitate to dispute it. Your credit report is like your financial report card, so it is crucial to make sure it is accurate.

Alright, that is the lowdown on maintaining good credit practices. It might seem like a lot to keep track of, but with a little effort and discipline, you can keep your credit score on the up and up. Remember, it is all about consistency and responsible use of credit. You have got this!'

When to seek professional credit repair help

Alright, let's talk about when it is time to call in the cavalry – professional credit repair help. Look, I get it. Sometimes, no matter how hard you try, you hit a wall with your credit. And that is totally normal! It happens to the best of us. But knowing when to seek help can make all the difference.

Here's the deal: if you find yourself feeling overwhelmed or stuck in a rut with your credit repair efforts, it might be time to enlist the expertise of professionals. Think of it like this – if your car breaks down, you would not try to fix it yourself if You are not a mechanic, right? Same goes for your credit

So, when exactly should you consider reaching out for help? Well, here are a few signs to watch out for:

- You are Feeling Overwhelmed: If You are drowning in a sea of credit card statements, collection notices, and confusing credit reports, it might be time to hand the reins over to someone who knows their stuff.
- You are Not Seeing Progress: Despite your best efforts, your credit score just will not budge. You are making payments on time, keeping your balances low, but nothing seems to be changing. That is a sign that you might need some professional guidance to get back on track.
- You are Facing Legal Issues: If You are dealing with legal issues related to your credit, like identity theft or inaccurate information on your credit report, it is definitely time to bring in the pros. They will know the ins and outs of the law and can help you navigate the murky waters of credit disputes.
- You are Not Sure Where to Start: Let's face it – credit repair can be confusing. If You are not sure where to start or what steps to take next, a professional can provide you with a roadmap to success.

Remember, seeking professional help is not a sign of failure – it isa smart move to help you get back on track with your finances. So, do not hesitate to reach out if you need it. Your credit is too important to leave to chance!

CHAPTER 6:
MANAGING DEBT RESPONSIBLY

You are standing at the edge of a financial abyss, staring down a mountain of debt that seems insurmountable. It is a daunting sight, one that millions of people around the world can relate to. But fear not, dear reader, for in this chapter, we will unravel the mysteries of managing debt responsibly and navigating your way to financial freedom.

Let me take you back to a time when debt had me in its grip, squeezing tighter with each passing day. I was fresh out of college, armed with a degree and a mountain of student loans to match. Like many young adults, I found myself juggling multiple debts – credit cards, car loans, you name it. It was overwhelming, to say the least. But through trial and error, I learned valuable lessons about debt management that I'm eager to share with you today.

When it comes to personal finance, one metric stands out as a beacon of insight into our financial health: the debt-to-income ratio (DTI). This numerical representation is not merely a figure on a spreadsheet but a window into our financial habits, decisions, and ultimately, our creditworthiness. Simply put, DTI is a measure of your monthly debt payments relative to your monthly income. To calculate it, add up all your monthly debt payments – including mortgage, car loans, credit card minimums, and student loans – and divide that sum by your gross monthly income. The resulting percentage is your DTI.

At its core, the debt-to-income ratio (DTI) is a measure of our financial obligations relative to our income. It paints a picture of how much of our earnings are consumed by debt payments, providing lenders with a snapshot of our ability to manage additional financial responsibilities. Calculating DTI involves a straightforward formula:

DTI = Total Monthly Debt Payments / Gross Monthly Income

Now, let's decipher the significance behind the numbers. While there's no one-size-fits-all answer, generally, lower DTI ratios are indicative of healthier financial habits. A DTI below 36% is often considered ideal, as it suggests that a manageable portion of our income is allocated towards debt repayment. This signifies a balanced approach to borrowing and a strong foundation for financial stability.

How Lenders Use DTI to Assess Your Creditworthiness

But why does DTI matter to lenders? Well, it serves as a critical tool in their assessment of our creditworthiness. Lenders use DTI to gauge our capacity to take on additional debt responsibly. A high DTI may signal potential risk, indicating that a significant portion of our income is already committed to debt payments. This could raise concerns about our ability to meet future financial obligations and may impact our eligibility for loans or credit lines.

Conversely, a low DTI paints a favorable picture, demonstrating that we have ample room in our budget to accommodate new debt responsibly. Lenders may view borrowers with low DTI ratios as less risky and more likely to honor their financial commitments, potentially leading to more favorable terms and interest rates.

In essence, DTI serves as a compass guiding lenders through the vast seas of financial data, helping them navigate the risks and rewards of extending credit. By understanding and managing our DTI effectively, we can enhance our creditworthiness, open doors to new financial opportunities, and chart a course towards a brighter financial future.

Strategies for Debt Repayment

Now that we have got a handle on understanding our debt, let's talk about how to tackle it head-on. There are several strategies you can employ, each with its own merits. Whether you are facing a towering mountain of debt or just a few pesky molehills, these methods will help you conquer your financial challenges with confidence and determination.

Debt Avalanche vs. Debt Snowball

Picture this: You are standing at the foot of a mountain, armed with nothing but a pickaxe and a map to guide you to the summit. The debt avalanche method is like taking the direct route – you tackle your debts in order of highest to lowest interest rates. By focusing on the debts with the highest interest rates first, you can save money on interest over time and pay off your debts more efficiently.

On the other hand, the debt snowball method is like forging your own path through the wilderness. You start by tackling the smallest debts first, regardless of interest rate, and work your way up from there. While this approach may not save you as much money on interest in the long run, it can provide a psychological boost as you knock out smaller debts and gain momentum.

So which method is right for you? It ultimately depends on your financial goals and personal preferences. The debt avalanche may be more financially efficient, but the debt snowball can provide a sense of accomplishment and motivation as you see quick wins along the way.

Now let us talk about budgeting – the unsung hero of debt repayment. Think of your budget as a roadmap that guides you toward your financial goals. Start by tracking your income and expenses to get a clear picture of where your money is going each month. Look for areas where you can cut back – do you really need that daily latte or monthly subscription box?

Consider implementing the envelope system, where you allocate cash to different spending categories and only spend what's in each envelope. Or try the zero-based budgeting method, where every dollar has a job – whether it is for bills, savings, or debt repayment. By being intentional and strategic with your spending, you can free up extra funds to put toward your debts.

Importance of Prioritizing High-Interest Debt:

Now let's talk about the elephant in the room – high-interest debt. It is like a ball and chain dragging you down, weighing heavily on your financial future. By prioritizing high-interest debt, you can minimize the amount of money you are throwing away on interest payments and accelerate your journey toward debt freedom.

Take a look at your debts and identify the ones with the highest interest rates – typically credit cards and personal loans. These are the debts that are costing you the most money each month, so it makes sense to tackle them first. By focusing your efforts on paying off high-interest debt, you can save yourself a significant amount of money in the long run and get out of debt faster.

Remember, tackling debt is a marathon, not a sprint. It requires patience, discipline, and perseverance. But by choosing the right repayment strategy, mastering the art of budgeting, and prioritizing high-interest debt, you can conquer your financial challenges and pave the way to a brighter, debt-free future.

Consolidation and Refinancing Options

In the world of debt management, consolidation and refinancing stand out as beacons of hope amidst the sea of financial challenges. These two strategies offer a glimmer of light to those navigating the murky waters of debt, providing avenues for relief and progress. Let us delve into the nuances of consolidation and refinancing, seeking to unravel their intricacies with both academic rigor and compassionate insight.

Consolidation, as the name implies, involves amalgamating multiple debts into a single, more manageable entity. It is akin to weaving a tapestry from disparate threads, creating a unified whole out of fragmented parts. By consolidating debts, individuals can streamline their repayment process, simplifying their financial obligations and potentially reducing the burden of high-interest rates.

Refinancing, on the other hand, offers a pathway to improved terms and conditions for existing loans. It is like renovating a house to enhance its value and functionality. Through refinancing, borrowers have the opportunity to secure lower interest rates, extend repayment periods, or even change the structure of their loans to better align with their financial goals.

But as with any financial decision, consolidation and refinancing come with their own set of considerations and caveats. While these options can offer relief in the form of lower monthly payments or reduced interest rates, they may also entail certain costs and risks. It is crucial for individuals to weigh the pros and cons carefully, considering factors such as fees, terms, and long-term implications before proceeding.

Moreover, consolidation and refinancing are not one-size-fits-all solutions. Their suitability depends on individual circumstances, including the types of debts involved, current interest rates, credit scores, and future financial plans. What works for one person may not necessarily be the best option for another. It is important to approach these decisions with a clear understanding of one's own financial situation and objectives.

In contemplating consolidation or refinancing, individuals should also be mindful of their broader financial landscape. These strategies are tools, not remedies, and should be integrated into a comprehensive debt management plan that addresses underlying financial habits and goals. Sustainable debt management requires more than just rearranging numbers on a balance sheet – it demands introspection, discipline, and a commitment to long-term financial well-being.

Ultimately, consolidation and refinancing hold the promise of relief and progress for those burdened by debt. They offer a lifeline to individuals striving to regain control of their financial futures, providing opportunities for consolidation, growth, and renewal. By approaching these options with both academic rigor and compassionate insight, we can illuminate the path to financial empowerment and inspire others to embark on their own journey towards debt freedom.

Avoiding Common Debt Traps

Let us shine a light on some of the most common debt traps lurking in the shadows, while also offering insights and strategies to help you steer clear of them.

Impulsive Spending:

The siren song of instant gratification – it is a temptation we've all faced at one time or another. Whether it is that shiny new gadget beckoning from the store shelf or the allure of a spontaneous shopping spree online, impulsive spending can quickly spiral out of control and land us knee-deep in debt. But fear not, for awareness is the first step towards overcoming this trap. By cultivating mindfulness in our spending habits and pausing to reflect on the true value of our purchases, we can resist the pull of impulse and make more informed financial decisions.

Lifestyle Inflation:

As our income grows, so too can our expenses – it isa phenomenon known as lifestyle inflation, and it can quietly chip away at our financial stability if left unchecked. From upgrading to a fancier car or indulging in lavish dining experiences, it is easy to fall into the trap of continually increasing our standard of living to match our income. But herein lies the danger – as our expenses balloon, so does our reliance on debt to sustain our lifestyle. By practicing moderation and prioritizing saving and debt repayment over extravagant expenditures, we can avoid the pitfalls of lifestyle inflation and build a more resilient financial future.

Overreliance on Credit:

In a world where credit cards and loans offer instant access to funds, it is all too easy to fall into the trap of overreliance on credit. From using credit cards to cover everyday expenses to taking out loans for non-essential purchases, relying too heavily on credit can quickly lead to a cycle of debt that is difficult to break free from. But here's the thing – credit should be a tool, not a crutch. By setting clear boundaries for ourselves and using credit responsibly, we can avoid the trap of overreliance and maintain control over our financial destiny.

Neglecting to Build an Emergency Fund:

Life is full of unexpected twists and turns – from medical emergencies to car repairs, you never know when a financial curveball might come your way. Yet, all too often, we neglect to build a safety net to catch us when we fall. Without an emergency fund to cushion the blow, we may find ourselves turning to credit cards or loans to cover unforeseen expenses, further exacerbating our debt burden. But by making saving a priority and setting aside a portion of our income each month for emergencies, we can protect ourselves from financial turmoil and reduce our reliance on debt as a fallback option.

Avoiding common debt traps requires a combination of awareness, discipline, and proactive planning. By recognizing the warning signs of impulsive spending, resisting lifestyle inflation, using credit responsibly, and prioritizing the building of an emergency fund, we can navigate the treacherous waters of debt with confidence and resilience.

In conclusion, managing debt responsibly requires a combination of knowledge, discipline, and strategic planning. By understanding your debt-to-income ratio, employing effective repayment strategies, exploring consolidation, and refinancing options, and avoiding common debt traps, you can take control of your financial destiny and pave the way to a brighter, debt-free future.

Arm yourself with these tools and embark on your journey to conquer the peaks of debt with confidence and determination. The path may be challenging, but the rewards – financial freedom, peace of mind, and a brighter future – are well worth the effort. Safe travels, and may your debts soon be but a distant memory on the horizon.

CHAPTER 7: CREDIT MONITORING AND PROTECTION

In the vast landscape of personal finance, where every dollar earned and spent holds the key to one's financial destiny, there exists a silent sentinel – a vigilant guardian standing watch over your most valuable asset: your credit. We embark on a journey into the heart of financial security, armed with knowledge, awareness, and the tools to safeguard our most precious asset against the ever-present threats of identity theft and fraud. In this chapter, we will explore the importance of credit monitoring, unravel the intricacies of identity theft and fraud protection, delve into the world of credit report freezes, and empower ourselves with the wisdom to navigate the complex landscape of credit monitoring services. So, buckle up, dear reader, for we are about to embark on a quest for financial resilience and peace of mind in the face of adversity.

In today's digital age, where information travels at the speed of light and data breaches are a dime a dozen, monitoring your credit is no longer just a good idea – it is an absolute necessity for safeguarding your financial security. Think of credit monitoring as your early warning system, alerting you to any suspicious activity or unauthorized changes to your credit report before they spiral out of control. By staying informed about changes to your credit profile, you can spot potential red flags and take swift action to mitigate any damage.

Let us dive into the importance of credit monitoring, breaking down why it is crucial for financial security, the benefits of staying informed about changes to your credit report, and how it can help detect and prevent identity theft.

What credit monitoring does

Credit monitoring services function by continuously observing and analyzing your credit information. They notify you of any modifications detected in your credit report via email, text message, or phone call. While individuals can manually monitor their credit, these services offer an automated and expedited approach to monitoring changes to their detailed credit profiles.

The specific activities monitored by credit monitoring services can vary among providers but typically encompass the following:

- Recording hard inquiries made on your credit report, such as those resulting from credit applications made in your name.
- Identifying newly opened accounts in your name.
- Tracking balances and payments on your credit accounts.
- Monitoring changes in personal information, including addresses and names, within your credit file.
- Alerting you to public records, such as bankruptcy filings, associated with your credit profile.
- Monitoring for the presence of personal information on the dark web, including your social security number, email address, and passwords.

While credit monitoring services offer comprehensive monitoring, it is important to note that they have limitations. Below, we elaborate on areas where credit monitoring may not provide complete coverage.

Why Monitoring Your Credit is Crucial for Financial Security:

Credit monitoring acts as your financial watchdog, keeping a vigilant eye on your credit report for any signs of suspicious activity. By regularly monitoring your credit, you can:

- **Detect unauthorized activity**: Spotting unfamiliar accounts or inquiries on your credit report can be an early warning sign of identity theft or fraudulent activity. By catching these red flags early, you can take swift action to protect your financial accounts and minimize potential damage.

- **Identify errors:** Credit reports aren't infallible – errors and inaccuracies can creep in from time to time. Monitoring your credit allows you to spot these errors and dispute them with the credit bureaus before they negatively impact your credit score.
- **Track your financial progress:** Monitoring your credit provides insight into your financial health and allows you to track changes in your credit score over time. It is like having a financial fitness tracker, helping you stay on top of your credit goals and make informed decisions about your financial future.

Credit monitoring, though a valuable tool for detecting potential fraud indicators, falls short of providing comprehensive protection against identity theft and unauthorized transactions.

Upon enrollment in credit monitoring services, subscribers gain access to alerts and resources aimed at recognizing and safeguarding against potential theft. However, it is important to note that these services do not offer a foolproof guarantee against fraud prevention. Instead, they serve to promptly notify individuals of suspicious activities, enabling them to take corrective measures swiftly.

Outlined below are several limitations of credit monitoring:

- Inability to prevent someone from applying for credit or opening new accounts using your identity.
- Lack of safeguarding against data breaches that may compromise your information.
- Incapacity to prevent credit card skimming incidents.
- Failure to notify you of unauthorized withdrawals from your bank account.
- Inability to alert you if someone files a tax return in your name and claims your refund.
- Insufficiency in preventing phishing emails targeting your personal information.

- Inability to directly report instances of fraud.
- Incapability to rectify errors on your credit report.
- Lack of capability to freeze your credit to prevent unauthorized access.
- It is essential to recognize these limitations and consider supplementary measures beyond credit monitoring for comprehensive protection against identity theft and fraud.

Benefits of Staying Informed About Changes to Your Credit Report:

Staying informed about changes to your credit report offers a host of benefits, including:

- **Early detection of fraud**: Credit monitoring alerts you to any significant changes or suspicious activity on your credit report, such as new accounts opened in your name or unauthorized inquiries. By receiving real-time alerts, you can take immediate action to investigate and address potential fraud before it escalates.
- **Protection against identity theft:** Identity thieves often target individuals with good credit scores, as they represent lucrative targets for fraudulent activity. By monitoring your credit regularly, you can detect and prevent identity theft before it wreaks havoc on your financial life.
- **Peace of mind:** Knowing that your credit is being monitored 24/7 provides peace of mind and reassurance that You are taking proactive steps to protect your financial security. It is like having a security blanket wrapped around your finances, allowing you to rest easy knowing that You are prepared for whatever life throws your way.

How Credit Monitoring Can Help Detect and Prevent Identity Theft:

Credit monitoring serves as a vital tool in the fight against identity theft, offering several key benefits:

- **Early detection:** Credit monitoring alerts you to any suspicious activity on your credit report, such as unauthorized account openings or sudden drops in your credit score. By detecting these warning signs early, you can take swift action to mitigate the impact of identity theft and prevent further damage to your credit.

- **Fraud prevention:** By monitoring your credit regularly, you can identify and address potential vulnerabilities in your financial accounts before they're exploited by identity thieves. Whether it is weak passwords, outdated security measures, or unauthorized access to your personal information, credit monitoring helps you stay one step ahead of the fraudsters.

- **Timely resolution:** In the unfortunate event that you become a victim of identity theft, credit monitoring can help streamline the resolution process by providing documentation of fraudulent activity and facilitating communication with creditors and credit bureaus. By acting quickly to dispute unauthorized charges and fraudulent accounts, you can minimize the long-term impact on your credit and financial stability.

In essence, credit monitoring is a proactive measure that empowers you to take control of your financial security and protect yourself against the ever-present threat of identity theft and fraud. By staying informed about changes to your credit report, you can detect suspicious activity early, prevent unauthorized access to your financial accounts, and safeguard your financial future for years to come.

Identity Theft and Fraud Protection

When individuals engage in identity theft, they unlawfully obtain your personal or financial details. Subsequently, they exploit this information to open credit card accounts or secure loans in your name, benefiting financially while leaving you accountable for the expenses.

Moreover, identity thieves may fraudulently submit a tax return using your identity in hopes of intercepting your tax refund. They could also infiltrate your credit card accounts to make substantial purchases or gain access to your online banking credentials to make unauthorized transactions.

It is imperative to promptly detect instances of identity theft to mitigate potential financial harm. Employing credit monitoring and identity theft protection services are effective strategies for identifying suspicious activity indicative of identity theft.

Identity theft is a pervasive threat in today's digital age, with cybercriminals constantly devising new and sophisticated methods to steal personal information and exploit unsuspecting victims. Understanding the common tactics used by identity thieves is crucial for protecting yourself and your financial security

Identity theft refers to the malicious act of seizing an individual's personal or financial details by nefarious actors. These perpetrators leverage the stolen information to engage in various fraudulent activities, such as opening unauthorized credit card accounts or obtaining loans under the victim's name, thereby reaping the financial gains while burdening the victim with ensuing liabilities.

In addition to this, identity thieves may resort to filing false tax returns to intercept the victim's income tax refunds, infiltrating credit card accounts to initiate substantial purchases, or gaining access to online banking platforms to conduct unauthorized transactions, depleting the victim's funds.

Detecting identity theft promptly is imperative to mitigate potential financial harm. Timely identification of such incidents can help prevent extensive damage inflicted by criminals.

In the unfortunate event of falling victim to identity theft, the Federal Trade Commission (FTC) advises taking specific measures to initiate the recovery process:

- Contact your credit card issuer or bank immediately if unauthorized access to your accounts has occurred. Similarly, communicate with any lenders or credit card companies that identity thieves have contacted to initiate fraudulent transactions.
- Implement a fraud alert and procure your credit reports. Utilize platforms like AnnualCreditReport.com to acquire complimentary credit reports, facilitating the detection of unauthorized loans or credit card accounts established in your name.
- Report the incident to the FTC. It is crucial to document cases of identity theft, as this report can serve as crucial evidence when disputing unauthorized charges or fraudulent loans associated with your identity.

Common Methods Used by Identity Thieves:

Identity thieves employ a variety of tactics to steal personal information, including:

Phishing scams: These fraudulent emails, texts, or phone calls masquerade as legitimate communications from trusted institutions, such as banks or government agencies, and attempt to trick individuals into divulging sensitive information like passwords, Social Security numbers, or account numbers.

Data breaches: Cybercriminals target businesses, government agencies, and other organizations to gain unauthorized access to vast troves of personal information, including names, addresses, Social Security numbers, and financial account numbers.

Skimming devices: These small, covert devices are used to capture credit or debit card information from unsuspecting victims when they swipe their cards at compromised ATMs, gas pumps, or point-of-sale terminals.

Dumpster diving: Identity thieves rummage through trash bins or recycling bins in search of discarded documents containing sensitive information, such as bank statements, credit card statements, or pre-approved credit offers.

Steps to Take if You Suspect You Have Been a Victim of Identity Theft:

If you suspect you have been a victim of identity theft, it is crucial to take immediate action to mitigate the damage and protect your financial accounts. Here are some steps you can take:

- Contact the fraud departments of the three major credit bureaus (Equifax, Experian, and TransUnion) to place a fraud alert on your credit report. This alert notifies potential creditors to take extra precautions when verifying your identity before extending credit in your name.
- File a report with the Federal Trade Commission (FTC) at IdentityTheft.gov, providing details about the identity theft and any fraudulent activity associated with your accounts.
- Contact your financial institutions and credit card issuers to report the identity theft and request that they freeze or close any affected accounts.
- Monitor your financial accounts and credit reports regularly for any suspicious activity, and report any unauthorized charges or accounts to the appropriate authorities.

Tips for Protecting Yourself from Fraud:

Prevention is the best defense against identity theft and fraud. Here are some tips for safeguarding your personal information and financial accounts:

- Shred sensitive documents before disposing of them, especially those containing personal information like Social Security numbers, account numbers, or passwords.
- Use strong, unique passwords for your online accounts, and enable two-factor authentication whenever possible to add an extra layer of security.
- Be cautious when sharing personal information online or over the phone, especially in response to unsolicited requests or communications from unfamiliar sources.
- Monitor your financial accounts regularly for any unauthorized transactions or suspicious activity, and report any discrepancies to your financial institution immediately.

Consider enrolling in identity theft protection services or credit monitoring services, which can provide added peace of mind and alert you to potential threats to your financial security.

In summary, protecting yourself from identity theft and fraud requires vigilance, awareness, and proactive measures to safeguard your personal information and financial accounts. By understanding the common methods used by identity thieves, taking prompt action if you suspect you have been a victim of identity theft, and following best practices for protecting your personal information, you can reduce the risk of falling victim to fraud and safeguard your financial security for years to come.

Freezing and thawing your credit report:

A credit report freeze, also known as a security freeze, is a proactive measure you can take to restrict access to your credit report. When you place a freeze on your credit report, potential creditors and lenders are unable to access your credit report or extend credit in your name without your explicit authorization. This can help prevent identity thieves from opening fraudulent accounts in your name and protect your financial security.

When It Might Be Appropriate to Freeze Your Credit:

There are several situations in which it might be appropriate to consider freezing your credit report:

- If you have been a victim of identity theft or suspect that your personal information has been compromised.
- If you are concerned about the security of your personal information following a data breach or security incident.
- If you are not planning to apply for new credit in the near future and want to proactively protect yourself against unauthorized access to your credit report.
- It is important to note that placing a freeze on your credit report does not impact your existing accounts or credit score, nor does it prevent you from accessing your own credit report or obtaining your credit score.

Process for Freezing and Thawing Your Credit Report with the Major Credit Bureaus:

The process for freezing and thawing your credit report with the major credit bureaus – Equifax, Experian, and TransUnion – is relatively straightforward and can typically be completed online, over the phone, or by mail. Here's how it works:

a. Contact each of the three major credit bureaus individually to request a credit report freeze. You may need to provide personal information to verify your identity, such as your name, address, Social Security number, and date of birth.

b. Once your credit report freeze is in place, potential creditors and lenders will be unable to access your credit report without your authorization. Keep in mind that you'll need to lift the freeze temporarily if you apply for new credit or need to authorize a credit check for other purposes.

c. To temporarily lift or "thaw" your credit report freeze, you will need to contact each of the three major credit bureaus and provide them with the necessary authorization. This typically involves providing a unique PIN or password that you received when you initially placed the freeze on your credit report.

d. After verifying your identity and confirming your request, the credit bureaus will temporarily lift the freeze on your credit report, allowing potential creditors and lenders to access your credit report for a specified period.

e. Once the specified period has elapsed or the purpose for lifting the freeze has been fulfilled, the credit bureaus will re-impose the freeze on your credit report, ensuring continued protection against unauthorized access.

Freezing and thawing your credit report is a proactive measure you can take to protect yourself against identity theft and unauthorized access to your credit report. By understanding the process and taking appropriate action, when necessary, you can safeguard your financial security and enjoy greater peace of mind knowing that your personal information is under lock and key.

Overview of Credit Monitoring Services:

Credit monitoring services are designed to help individuals keep track of their credit health and detect any suspicious activity that may indicate identity theft or fraud. These services typically offer a range of features, including:

- Monitoring of your credit report from one or more of the major credit bureaus (Equifax, Experian, and TransUnion) for changes or discrepancies.

- Real-time alerts via email, text message, or mobile app notifications whenever there is a significant change to your credit report, such as a new account opening, a late payment, or a change in your credit score.
- Access to your credit score and credit report on a regular basis, allowing you to track changes over time and identify areas for improvement.
- Identity theft insurance or reimbursement coverage to help cover the costs associated with resolving identity theft or fraudulent activity.

Features to Look for When Choosing a Credit Monitoring Service:

When selecting a credit monitoring service, it is important to consider the following factors:

- **Coverage:** Ensure that the service monitors your credit report with all three major credit bureaus to provide comprehensive protection.
- **Frequency of Monitoring:** Look for a service that offers continuous monitoring of your credit report, as well as real-time alerts for any significant changes.
- **Alert Customization:** Choose a service that allows you to customize the types of alerts you receive and the methods of notification (email, text, etc.).
- **Identity Theft Protection:** Opt for a service that includes identity theft insurance or reimbursement coverage to provide added peace of mind.
- **Ease of Use:** Select a service with a user-friendly interface and intuitive features that make it easy to access your credit information and understand alerts.

How to Interpret and Respond to Alerts from Credit Monitoring Services:

When you receive an alert from your credit monitoring service, it is important to take prompt action to investigate and address any potential issues. Here is how to interpret and respond to alerts effectively:

Review the alert carefully to understand the nature of the change or discrepancy in your credit report.

Log in to your credit monitoring service's platform to access additional details about the alert, including which credit bureau(s) detected the change and when it occurred.

Verify the accuracy of the information and determine whether it was the result of legitimate activity or potential fraud.

If you suspect fraudulent activity, take immediate steps to protect your identity and financial accounts, such as placing a fraud alert on your credit report, notifying your financial institutions, and filing a report with the Federal Trade Commission (FTC) at *IdentityTheft.gov.*

Follow up with the credit monitoring service to confirm that the alert has been resolved and to ensure that your credit report is accurate and up-to-date.

In summary, credit monitoring services are valuable tools for helping individuals protect their credit health and detect potential signs of identity theft or fraud. By choosing a reputable service with comprehensive features and taking proactive steps to interpret and respond to alerts, you can stay one step ahead of cybercriminals and safeguard your financial security for the long term.

CHAPTER 8: ADVANCED TOPICS IN CREDIT MANAGEMENT

Standing on the precipice of possibility, armed with the knowledge and strategies to navigate the labyrinth of credit mastery with finesse and confidence. As you step into this realm of advanced credit management, prepare to be swept away on a journey of discovery, where the secrets to unlocking unparalleled financial potential await.

In this chapter, we transcend the ordinary and delve into the extraordinary – exploring advanced strategies that will revolutionize your approach to credit management and propel you toward unparalleled financial success. From negotiating with creditors to understanding bankruptcy, rebuilding credit after financial hardship, and unlocking the full potential of your credit profile, each section is a gateway to new horizons of financial empowerment.

This is a roadmap to financial freedom, and a testament to the power of knowledge and determination. So, dear reader, fasten your seatbelt and prepare to embark on a journey that will challenge your perceptions, ignite your passion for financial mastery, and ultimately transform your relationship with credit forever. Get ready to unleash the full force of your financial potential and embark on a quest for prosperity, abundance, and freedom. The adventure begins now.

Negotiation emerges as a powerful tool – a skillful interplay between borrower and lender that can shape the trajectory of one's financial future. Negotiating with creditors is not just about haggling over terms; it is about advocating for your financial interests, leveraging your position, and forging mutually beneficial agreements that pave the way for financial stability and success. Here, we will delve into the art of negotiation, exploring proven strategies, real-life examples, and practical tips for negotiating with creditors with confidence and finesse.

Strategies for Negotiating with Creditors

- Know Your Financial Situation:

Before entering into negotiations with creditors, it is essential to have a clear understanding of your financial situation. Take stock of your income, expenses, debts, and assets to assess your financial health and determine what you can realistically afford to pay. This information will serve as the foundation for your negotiation strategy.

- Open Communication:

Effective negotiation begins with open and honest communication. Reach out to your creditors proactively to discuss your financial challenges and explore potential solutions. Be transparent about your circumstances, and express your willingness to work together to find a mutually acceptable resolution.

- Offer a Compromise:

When negotiating with creditors, it is often helpful to offer a compromise that benefits both parties. For example, you may propose a reduced payment plan, a lower interest rate, or the waiving of late fees or penalties in exchange for a commitment to repay the debt over time. By demonstrating your willingness to cooperate and meet your obligations, you can build goodwill and strengthen your negotiating position.

- Seek Professional Assistance:

If you are struggling to negotiate with creditors on your own, consider seeking professional assistance from a credit counseling agency or a debt settlement firm. These organizations have experience negotiating with creditors on behalf of consumers and can help you navigate the negotiation process more effectively.

Examples of Successful Negotiation

Lowering Interest Rates:

Jane, a credit card holder, was struggling to keep up with her monthly payments due to high-interest rates. She contacted her credit card company and explained her financial hardship, requesting a lower interest rate. After reviewing her account history and financial situation, the credit card company agreed to reduce her interest rate, making it easier for her to manage her debt.

Setting Up a Payment Plan:

John, a homeowner facing foreclosure, reached out to his mortgage lender to discuss his options. Instead of proceeding with foreclosure proceedings, the lender agreed to work with John to set up a repayment plan that allowed him to catch up on missed payments over time. By negotiating a payment plan, John was able to avoid foreclosure and protect his home.

Tools for Effective Negotiation

- Documentation:

Keep detailed records of all communications with creditors, including phone calls, emails, and letters. Document any agreements or promises made during negotiations to ensure accountability and protect your rights.

- Patience and Persistence:

Negotiating with creditors can be a lengthy and sometimes frustrating process, but patience and persistence are key. Do not be afraid to follow up with creditors regularly and advocate for your interests until a resolution is reached.

Negotiating with creditors is a fundamental skill in the realm of credit management, offering the opportunity to advocate for your financial interests and find mutually beneficial solutions to financial challenges. By employing strategies such as open communication, compromise, and seeking professional assistance when needed, you can navigate the negotiation process with confidence and achieve positive outcomes that pave the way for financial stability and success.

Bankruptcy and Its Effects on Credit

Bankruptcy – a word laden with weight and consequence, yet often seen as a last resort for individuals grappling with overwhelming debt and financial hardship. But what are the implications of bankruptcy on one's creditworthiness and financial future?

Bankruptcy is a legal process designed to provide individuals and businesses with a fresh start by eliminating or restructuring their debts under the protection of the bankruptcy court.

There are several types of bankruptcy, with C7 and C13 being the most common for individuals:

- C7 bankruptcy, also known as liquidation bankruptcy, involves the sale of non-exempt assets to repay creditors, with remaining debts typically discharged (eliminated) at the end of the process.
- C13 bankruptcy, often referred to as reorganization bankruptcy, involves creating a repayment plan to pay off debts over a period of three to five years, with any remaining eligible debts discharged upon successful completion of the plan.

Effects of Bankruptcy on Credit:

The effects of bankruptcy on credit can be profound and long-lasting, impacting credit scores, credit reports, and overall creditworthiness:

- Credit Scores: Bankruptcy can cause a significant drop in credit scores, as it is viewed as a negative event by credit scoring models. The extent of the score decrease depends on various factors, including the type of bankruptcy, the individual's credit history prior to bankruptcy, and the presence of other derogatory marks on their credit report.
- Credit Reports: Bankruptcy remains on credit reports for a significant period, typically seven to ten years for C7 bankruptcy and seven years for C13 bankruptcy. During this time, the bankruptcy notation can make it difficult to obtain new credit or loans, and may result in higher interest rates or less favorable terms when credit is extended.
- Creditworthiness: Bankruptcy can have broader implications for creditworthiness beyond credit scores and reports, affecting one's ability to qualify for housing, employment, insurance, and other financial opportunities that rely on a positive credit history.

Navigating the Aftermath of Bankruptcy:

While bankruptcy can have serious consequences for credit, it is not the end of the road for financial recovery. With time, diligence, and strategic planning, individuals can rebuild their credit and work toward a brighter financial future:

- Establish a Solid Financial Foundation: Start by creating a budget, building an emergency fund, and developing healthy financial habits to lay the groundwork for long-term financial stability.
- Monitor Credit Reports: Regularly review your credit reports from all three major credit bureaus (Equifax, Experian, and TransUnion) to ensure accuracy and identify any errors or discrepancies that may need to be addressed.
- Rebuild Credit Responsibly: Consider opening a secured credit card, becoming an authorized user on someone else's account,

or obtaining a small installment loan to begin rebuilding credit. Make timely payments and keep credit utilization low to demonstrate responsible credit management.

- Seek Professional Guidance: Consult with a reputable credit counselor or financial advisor who can provide personalized guidance and support tailored to your unique financial situation and goals.

Bankruptcy can have significant effects on credit, impacting credit scores, credit reports, and overall creditworthiness. However, with patience, perseverance, and strategic planning, individuals can navigate the aftermath of bankruptcy and rebuild their credit over time. By understanding the implications of bankruptcy, taking proactive steps to monitor credit, and seeking professional guidance when needed, you can chart a course toward financial recovery and reclaim your financial future with confidence and resilience.

Rebuilding Credit After Financial Hardship

In the intricate tapestry of personal finance, few challenges are as daunting as the journey of rebuilding credit after facing financial adversity. Whether you have experienced the devastating impact of bankruptcy, foreclosure, or overwhelming debt, the road to credit recovery is fraught with challenges and obstacles. Yet, within these challenges lies an opportunity for growth, resilience, and ultimately, redemption.

The first step in rebuilding credit after financial hardship is to establish a solid financial foundation upon which to build your future. This includes:

Creating a budget: Develop a comprehensive budget that outlines your income, expenses, and financial goals. Track your spending habits and identify areas where you can cut back or reallocate funds towards debt repayment and savings.

Building an emergency fund: Start setting aside funds in an emergency savings account to cover unexpected expenses and emergencies. Aim to save at least three to six months' worth of living expenses to provide a financial safety net in case of job loss, medical emergencies, or other unforeseen circumstances.

Implementing Targeted Credit Repair Tactics

With a solid financial foundation in place, it is time to tackle the task of repairing your credit and improving your credit score. This may involve:

Reviewing your credit report: Obtain copies of your credit reports from all three major credit bureaus (Equifax, Experian, and TransUnion) and carefully review them for errors or inaccuracies. Dispute any inaccuracies with the credit bureaus and work to have them corrected promptly.

Paying off outstanding debts: Develop a strategy for paying off outstanding debts, starting with high-interest debts or accounts in collections. Consider negotiating with creditors to settle debts for less than the full amount owed or setting up payment plans to repay debts over time.

Leveraging Alternative Credit-Building Tools:

In addition to traditional credit accounts, there are alternative credit-building tools that can help you establish or rebuild your credit history, such as:

- **Secured credit cards:** Secured credit cards require a security deposit as collateral and can be used to build or rebuild credit. Make small purchases with your secured card and pay off the balance in full each month to demonstrate responsible credit behavior.
- **Credit builder loans:** Credit builder loans are designed to help individuals build credit by making regular monthly payments.

These loans are typically offered by credit unions and community banks and may require a small deposit or upfront fee.

The journey of rebuilding credit after financial hardship is not an easy one, but it is a journey worth undertaking. By establishing a solid financial foundation, implementing targeted credit repair tactics, and leveraging alternative credit-building tools, you can overcome the challenges of financial adversity and reclaim your financial future with confidence and determination. Remember, the road to credit recovery may be long and arduous, but with patience, perseverance, and a steadfast commitment to your financial goals, you can emerge stronger and more resilient than ever before.

Understanding Credit Utilization

Credit cards have become an integral part of modern-day living, offering convenience, flexibility, and rewards to consumers worldwide. Yet, amidst the allure of instant gratification, lies a crucial factor that can significantly impact one's creditworthiness – credit utilization. Let's explore the dynamics of credit utilization, examine the benefits and risks of using credit cards for everyday expenses, and offer practical tips for responsible credit card use that can help you navigate the complexities of credit management with confidence and wisdom.

Benefits and Risks of Using Credit Cards

Credit cards offer a plethora of benefits that make them an attractive option for everyday spending. From earning cash back rewards and travel perks to enjoying purchase protection and convenience, credit cards can enhance your purchasing power and streamline your financial transactions. However, with great power comes great responsibility, and the risks associated with credit card use cannot be overlooked.

One of the primary risks of using credit cards is the temptation to overspend beyond one's means, leading to high balances and potential debt accumulation. Additionally, carrying high balances on credit cards can result in increased credit utilization ratios, which can negatively impact your credit score and decrease your creditworthiness in the eyes of lenders.

Furthermore, missed or late payments on credit card accounts can result in costly fees, penalty interest rates, and damage to your credit score. Therefore, it is essential to approach credit card use with caution and discipline, balancing the benefits of convenience and rewards with the potential risks of overspending and debt accumulation.

Tips for Responsible Credit Card Use:

1. Pay Your Balance in Full Each Month: One of the most effective ways to manage credit card debt and minimize interest charges is to pay your balance in full each month. By doing so, you can avoid carrying high balances and keep your credit utilization ratio low, which can have a positive impact on your credit score.

2. Keep Track of Your Spending: Monitoring your credit card spending regularly can help you stay on top of your finances and avoid overspending. Consider using budgeting tools or mobile apps to track your expenses and set spending limits to ensure you stay within your means.

3. Use Credit Cards Strategically: Instead of using credit cards for impulse purchases or non-essential expenses, consider using them strategically for planned purchases or to earn rewards on essential expenses like groceries or gas. This can help you maximize the benefits of credit card use while minimizing the risks of overspending.

4. Pay Your Bills on Time: Timely payment of your credit card bills is crucial for maintaining a positive payment history and avoiding late fees and penalty interest rates. Consider setting up automatic payments or reminders to ensure you never miss a payment deadline.

5. Regularly Monitor Your Credit Utilization: Keeping a close eye on your credit utilization ratio – the percentage of your available credit that You are using – can help you identify potential red flags and take corrective action if needed. Aim to keep your credit utilization below 30% to maintain a healthy credit score.

By balancing the benefits and risks of using credit cards for everyday expenses and implementing practical tips for responsible credit card use, you can harness the power of credit to enhance your financial well-being and achieve your long-term financial goals.

Credit Card Terms and Conditions

Credit card terms and conditions may seem like a maze of legalese and fine print, but understanding them is essential for navigating the credit card landscape effectively. From interest rates and fees to payment deadlines and credit limits, each aspect of a credit card agreement can have a profound impact on your financial health.

One key aspect to understand is the Annual Percentage Rate (APR), which represents the annualized cost of borrowing on a credit card. By familiarizing yourself with the APR and other fees associated with your credit card, such as annual fees, balance transfer fees, and late payment fees, you can make informed decisions about how and when to use your credit card responsibly.

Another important consideration is the grace period – the time between the end of a billing cycle and the due date for payment – during which you can pay your balance in full to avoid accruing interest charges. By paying your balance in full before the end of the grace period, you can minimize interest charges and maximize the benefits of using a credit card.

<u>Maximizing Credit Card Rewards:</u>

Credit card rewards programs offer a tantalizing array of benefits, from cash back and travel rewards to points and miles that can be redeemed for merchandise, gift cards, or statement credits. However, navigating the world of credit card rewards requires careful consideration of the terms, conditions, and redemption options available.

To maximize credit card rewards, it is essential to choose a rewards program that aligns with your spending habits and lifestyle preferences. Whether you prefer cash back on everyday purchases, travel rewards for frequent flyers, or points for specific categories like dining or groceries, there's a rewards program out there that is tailored to your needs.

Additionally, leveraging sign-up bonuses, bonus categories, and promotional offers can help you earn rewards more quickly and efficiently. By strategically timing your purchases to align with bonus categories or taking advantage of limited-time promotions, you can supercharge your rewards earnings and unlock new opportunities for financial benefits.

Avoiding Common Credit Card Traps and Pitfalls:

While credit cards offer a wealth of benefits, they also pose potential pitfalls for unwary consumers. From overspending and accruing high-interest debt to falling victim to fraud and identity theft, there are several common traps that credit card users should be aware of and avoid at all costs.

One common trap to avoid is carrying high balances on your credit cards, which can lead to increased credit utilization ratios and potentially damage your credit score. By paying your balance in full each month and avoiding unnecessary debt, you can mitigate the risk of overspending and keep your credit utilization low.

Another pitfall to watch out for is falling victim to credit card fraud or identity theft. By monitoring your credit card statements regularly for unauthorized charges, keeping your personal information secure, and reporting any suspicious activity to your card issuer immediately, you can protect yourself against fraud and minimize the impact on your financial health.

Advanced Strategies for Maximizing Your Credit Potential

Credit utilization is a key factor in determining your credit score, representing the ratio of your outstanding credit card balances to your total credit limits. Keeping your credit utilization low – ideally below 30% – demonstrates responsible credit management and can have a positive impact on your credit score. But beyond simply keeping your balances low, advanced strategies for maximizing credit utilization involve strategic timing and utilization patterns. For example, spreading out your credit card payments throughout the month to always keep your balances low or strategically timing large purchases to minimize their impact on your utilization ratio can help optimize your credit utilization and boost your credit score over time.

- **Diversifying Your Credit Mix:**

Another advanced strategy for maximizing your credit potential involves diversifying your credit mix – the types of credit accounts you have in your credit history. Lenders and credit scoring models typically prefer to see a diverse mix of credit accounts, including revolving credit (such as credit cards) and installment credit (such as mortgages, auto loans, or personal loans). By diversifying your credit mix, you demonstrate your ability to manage different types of credit responsibly, which can have a positive impact on your credit score. However, it is important to approach credit diversification strategically and avoid opening new accounts indiscriminately, as excessive credit inquiries or new accounts can have a negative impact on your credit score in the short term.

- **Optimizing Authorized User Accounts:**

Authorized user accounts are another powerful tool for maximizing your credit potential, allowing you to piggyback on the positive credit history of a family member or friend. By becoming an authorized user on an existing credit account with a long history of on-time payments and low balances, you can potentially boost your own credit score and establish a positive credit history more quickly. However, it is essential to choose the right account and ensure that the primary account holder maintains responsible credit habits, as any negative activity on the account could potentially harm your credit score as well.

Legal Rights and Credit Laws

From accessing accurate credit information to protecting against discrimination and billing errors, a robust system of laws and regulations exists to ensure fair treatment and empower consumers.

1. **Fair Credit Reporting Act (FCRA):**

The Fair Credit Reporting Act (FCRA) stands as a pillar of consumer protection, granting individuals crucial rights regarding their credit information. Under the FCRA, consumers have the right to access their credit reports from nationwide credit reporting agencies (CRAs) once every 12 months for free. Moreover, the FCRA mandates that CRAs maintain accurate and up-to-date credit information, investigate consumer disputes promptly, and correct any inaccuracies found.

For instance, if a consumer discovers an error on their credit report—such as an account erroneously marked as delinquent or a fraudulent account opened in their name—they have the right to dispute the information with the credit reporting agency. Through this process, consumers can ensure the integrity of their credit reports and protect their financial reputation.

2. **Equal Credit Opportunity Act (ECOA):**

The Equal Credit Opportunity Act (ECOA) serves as a critical safeguard against discrimination in credit transactions. Enforced by the Federal Trade Commission (FTC), the ECOA prohibits creditors from discriminating against credit applicants based on race, color, religion, national origin, sex, marital status, age, or receipt of public assistance. Additionally, the ECOA mandates that creditors evaluate credit applications based on factors such as creditworthiness and ability to repay, rather than discriminatory criteria.

For example, if an individual believes they were denied credit or offered less favorable terms based on a protected characteristic, they have the right to file a complaint with the appropriate regulatory agency, such as the Consumer Financial Protection Bureau (CFPB) or the FTC. By upholding the provisions of the ECOA, consumers can ensure fair and equitable treatment in credit transactions.

3. Fair Credit Billing Act (FCBA):

The Fair Credit Billing Act (FCBA) provides consumers with important protections against billing errors and unauthorized charges on their credit card accounts. Under the FCBA, consumers have the right to dispute billing errors within 60 days of receiving their credit card statement. During the dispute process, creditors are required to investigate the claim and correct any errors promptly. Additionally, consumers have the right to withhold payment on the disputed amount while the investigation is underway.

For instance, if a consumer identifies an unauthorized charge on their credit card statement or notices a billing error, they can notify the credit card issuer and request that the charge be removed or corrected. By exercising their rights under the FCBA, consumers can safeguard themselves against fraudulent charges and billing inaccuracies.

4. Consumer Financial Protection Bureau (CFPB) Regulations:

The Consumer Financial Protection Bureau (CFPB) plays a pivotal role in enforcing consumer protection laws and regulations related to financial products and services. Established in the aftermath of the 2008 financial crisis, the CFPB is tasked with overseeing various aspects of the financial industry, including mortgages, credit cards, student loans, and debt collection practices. The bureau investigates consumer complaints, conducts examinations of financial institutions, and takes enforcement action against companies that engage in unfair, deceptive, or abusive practices.

For example, if a consumer encounters an issue with a financial product or service—such as a billing dispute, debt collection harassment, or misleading advertising—they can file a complaint with the CFPB through its online complaint portal. The CFPB then investigates the complaint and works to resolve the issue, holding financial companies accountable for their actions and ensuring that consumers are treated fairly.

Harnessing Credit Monitoring and Management Tools

In today's digital age, technology has made it easier than ever to monitor and manage your credit effectively. Advanced credit monitoring and management tools, such as credit monitoring services, budgeting apps, and credit score simulators, provide valuable insights into your credit and financial health, while identifying areas for improvement. By leveraging these tools strategically, you can stay informed about changes to your credit report, track your credit score over time, and help you take proactive steps to optimize your credit potential.

At the same time, by delving into the intricacies of negotiating with creditors, understanding the complexities of bankruptcy, rebuilding credit after financial hardship, and exploring advanced credit management strategies, your knowledge, insight, and confidence will expand and you will have the necessary tools to navigate the complexities of credit management with ease and sophistication.

Lastly, mastering advanced strategies for maximizing your credit potential is the key to unlocking new opportunities for financial growth and prosperity. By understanding the details of credit utilization, coupled with diversifying your credit mix, optimizing authorized user accounts, and harnessing advanced credit monitoring and management tools, you will gain the knowledge and insights needed to elevate your credit game to new heights of mastery. So, my dear reader, embrace the journey ahead with open arms and a curious mind, for the adventure of credit mastery awaits.

CHAPTER 9: ADVANCED TOPICS IN CREDIT MANAGEMENT

A young couple, deeply in love and eager to embark on life's adventures together. In a whirlwind of excitement, they open a joint credit card account, symbolizing their commitment to shared dreams and financial unity. Yet, as the years pass, the relationship evolves, and unforeseen challenges arise. Eventually, the couple finds themselves navigating the complexities of separation and divorce, confronting the harsh reality of untangling their financial lives and grappling with the lasting impact on their creditworthiness.

As we journey through the chapters of this book, we will unravel the intricacies of credit and relationships, exploring the implications of joint accounts, co-signing, and the fallout of divorce and separation on credit scores. But that is just the beginning. Brace yourself as we delve deeper into the realm of credit and employment, uncovering the hidden connections between creditworthiness and job opportunities, insurance premiums, and renting decisions. Are you ready to embark on this transformative journey? Let's dive in.

Credit and Relationship

The intersection of credit and relationships can be both a source of strength and a potential minefield. Whether opening joint accounts, co-signing for loans, or navigating the aftermath of divorce or separation, the financial decisions made within relationships can have a lasting impact on individuals' creditworthiness and financial well-being.

Co-signing on a credit card account entails assuming financial liability to aid another individual in bolstering their credit standing. Nowadays, most banks have moved away from permitting co-signing on credit cards, favoring instead the option of authorized usership to assist individuals with limited credit in improving their financial standing, guided by someone with a more established credit history.

When someone co-signs on a credit account, they essentially agree to be accountable for the charges on the account if the primary account holder fails to meet payment obligations. Despite not being the primary account holder and not having access to the account, the co-signer provides a guarantee that they will step in if the primary holder cannot cover the bill.

Co-signing may be considered when the primary account holder would otherwise be denied due to poor or nonexistent credit history. Typically, the bank allows a co-signer to assume responsibility for any outstanding debt if the primary holder defaults on payments. While co-signing was once commonplace, it is now offered by only a few issuers. Co-signing for a credit card can be a beneficial option for individuals with low credit scores, including parents or guardians seeking to help their children establish credit. However, it is not always the optimal choice, as there are alternative solutions available. Like any financial decision, there are advantages and disadvantages to sharing the responsibility of a credit card account with another person. According to the regulations outlined in The CARD Act of 2009, a co-signer must be at least 21 years old, demonstrate the capacity to make minimum payments on the account, and possess sufficient creditworthiness to qualify for the credit card.

Advantages of Co-Signing

Enhanced Approval Odds and Better Terms

- Securing new credit cards can pose challenges for individuals with limited or poor credit histories, especially concerning cards offering appealing benefits and rewards.
- By co-signing for someone with credit challenges, your strong credit score can bolster their application, mitigating the lender's perceived risk during evaluation.

- Moreover, a combination of good credit and supplementary income may result in more favorable terms such as lower interest rates, increased credit limits, and overall better terms.

Potential Credit Boost for Both Parties

- Responsibly managed credit card usage has the potential to uplift credit scores for all parties involved. Conversely, mismanagement of credit card accounts can adversely affect the credit of both the primary account holder and the co-signer.

Disadvantages of Co-Signing

Credit Score Vulnerability

- Any instances of late or missed payments on the account are attributed to the co-signer, potentially impacting both parties' credit scores.
- Late payments or defaults can inflict significant harm on the credit scores of both the primary account holder and the co-signer.

Potential Limitation on Future Borrowing Capacity

- Despite having good credit, co-signing for credit card debt may hinder eligibility for future financing.
- Lenders assess your debt-to-income ratio (DTI) when considering new financing applications. A higher DTI resulting from an additional account can diminish borrowing capacity.

Risk of Strained Relationships

- Co-signing poses a significant risk to interpersonal relationships.

- For instance, co-signing for a child's credit card with certain understandings about responsible usage can lead to complications if the agreement is not upheld.
- Co-signers must remember that they are ultimately accountable for the debt, irrespective of any personal agreements with the other party. In the event of default, the co-signer is liable to settle the outstanding balance.

Distinguishing Co-Signing from Joint Credit Cards

Co-signing and joint credit card ownership are often conflated, but they entail distinct responsibilities. While a co-signer assumes debt risk without accessing the account, joint account holders share equal responsibility and full access to the account.

Joint Credit Cards

When opening a joint credit card, both parties accept equal liability for charges incurred on the account. Both individuals must submit applications and are granted the privileges and obligations of primary account holders. The account's activity and history are reflected on the credit reports of all joint account holders.

Alternatives to Co-Signing

Co-signing for credit cards has become increasingly rare. However, achieving the objectives typically associated with co-signing—such as assisting someone in building or accessing credit—can be accomplished through alternative means.

Secured Credit Cards

Secured credit cards provide a relatively straightforward method for building credit independently, without reliance on family or friends. Applicants over 21 years old who face credit challenges or lack credit history may benefit from a secured card's credit-building potential.

With a secured credit card, the cardholder submits a deposit equivalent to the credit limit, typically resulting in a one-to-one correlation. This deposit mitigates risk for the card issuer, facilitating easier qualification compared to unsecured cards, even for individuals with limited or poor credit history.

Authorized User

Authorized users, commonly offered by banks, entails issuing secondary cards tied to a primary user's account. Activity on these cards is typically reported to credit bureaus, making it a viable option for credit-building purposes.

Adding an authorized user may be beneficial for individuals who:

- Prefer streamlined budgeting via a shared credit card account.
- Seek to accumulate credit card rewards collectively.
- Encounter difficulty qualifying for a credit card independently due to credit issues.
- Require assistance in establishing credit for the first time.
- Although joint credit cards and co-signing are less prevalent, many credit card issuers permit adding authorized users to accounts. Authorized users receive separate cards but remain tied to the primary account, with activity potentially reported on their credit reports.

As the primary account holder, you retain control when authorizing others to use your account. You can remove authorized users at any time and remain responsible for their charges. However, authorized users generally lack the ability to request credit limit increases, add additional users, or dispute fraudulent transactions.

Adding a partner or child as an authorized user can achieve similar objectives as co-signing, with the risk more manageable and directly controllable for the primary account holder.

Co-signing for credit card accounts has become less common, necessitating careful consideration before pursuing this option. Exploring alternatives like secured credit cards and authorized usership can provide viable means of achieving credit-related goals while mitigating associated risks.

Impact of Divorce and Separation on Credit

Divorce and separation can introduce significant challenges to the financial lives of individuals, particularly when joint accounts or co-signed loans are involved. During the process of separating assets and liabilities, it is essential to take proactive steps to protect your credit score and financial interests.

One of the first steps is to close joint accounts or refinance co-signed loans to remove one partner's liability. Closing joint accounts prevents further accumulation of debt by either party and ensures that future financial transactions are separate. Refinancing co-signed loans allows the primary borrower to assume sole responsibility for the debt, relieving the co-signer of any obligations.

Additionally, it is crucial to monitor credit reports closely during and after the divorce or separation process. By staying vigilant, individuals can identify any discrepancies or unauthorized accounts that may arise as a result of the separation. Addressing these issues promptly can help prevent further damage to credit scores and ensure a smoother transition to financial independence.

The Importance of a Good Credit Score While Renting

Creditworthiness holds significant importance in various facets of life, including the process of renting a home. Prospective tenants often undergo scrutiny of their credit profiles by landlords or property managers during the application process. This scrutiny is aimed at assessing an individual's financial track record to gauge their potential reliability as a tenant. Thus, maintaining a favorable credit score becomes pivotal when seeking rental accommodations.

Landlords typically evaluate several aspects of an applicant's credit history. These include the overall credit score, payment history, instances of bankruptcies or foreclosures, and overall credit activity. Such scrutiny aims to ascertain the applicant's capability to fulfill rent obligations regularly and to address any potential liabilities arising from property damages.

While a lower credit score does not invariably result in rental denial, it prompts landlords to delve deeper into the circumstances contributing to the score. Although most landlords typically seek applicants with credit scores around 620 or higher, exceptions may exist based on individual circumstances.

In cases where applicants fall short of the minimum credit score requirements, alternative avenues may still facilitate lease acquisition:

- Transparent Communication: Honesty regarding one's credit history can foster understanding from landlords, especially when accompanied by valid reasons such as medical expenses or recent life transitions like divorce.
- Increased Security Deposit: Offering a higher security deposit provides landlords with added assurance, serving as a financial buffer in the event of payment defaults.
- References: Providing references from previous landlords can offer insights into one's reliability as a tenant, supplementing the assessment beyond the credit score.
- Cosigner Arrangement: Landlords may consider applicants with a cosigner, who assumes responsibility in case of payment defaults, thereby mitigating the perceived risk.
- Roommate Arrangement: Opting for a roommate can alleviate concerns about sole financial responsibility, potentially making the applicant a more appealing prospect to landlords.

- Advance Rent Payments: Offering to pay several months' rent upfront can instill confidence in landlords regarding the applicant's financial stability, thereby facilitating the rental agreement process.

In conclusion, while a good credit score significantly enhances one's prospects in securing rental accommodations, alternative arrangements and transparent communication can still pave the way for lease acquisition, even in cases of suboptimal credit scores.

Credit and Employment

When pursuing a new employment opportunity, there's more to consider beyond polishing your resume, crafting a compelling cover letter, and honing your interview skills. Prior to sending out your next job application, it is prudent to evaluate and potentially enhance your credit standing. Research from a 2018 HR.com study, supported by the National Association of Background Screeners (NABS), revealed that 95% of companies engage in some form of background screening for prospective hires. Among these, 16% routinely conduct credit or financial assessments on all candidates, with nearly a third opting for such checks on select individuals.

While prospective employers may review your credit history, it is crucial to note that, unlike financial institutions, they lack access to your credit score or specific account details. Dispelling a common misconception, it is important to understand precisely what information employers can access during a credit inquiry.

But why does your credit report matter to potential employers? Essentially, certain elements within the report can offer insights into habits or traits that might not align with their workplace culture. For instance, a pattern of overdue credit accounts could imply disorganization or a lack of reliability. Similarly, substantial debt or multiple credit cards nearing their limits might raise concerns about financial stability and potential risks of misconduct, such as theft or fraud. While it might seem as though employers are making judgments without fully understanding you, it is essential to recognize that the process of hiring and onboarding new personnel entails significant expenses. Thus, employers strive to minimize potential risks wherever possible.

An employment credit check provides a summary of your borrowing history, offering potential employers a tool for informed hiring decisions. Typically, companies conduct these checks either just prior to extending a formal job offer or after making a conditional offer.

It is uncommon for businesses to conduct credit checks on every single applicant due to the associated time and costs involved. In the majority of cases, the information gleaned from these checks primarily pertains to personal credit and debt. Some employers view an individual's financial management skills as indicative of their potential job performance.

Beyond assessing financial responsibility, credit reports can serve as a means to verify identity, validate educational and employment backgrounds, and mitigate risks of theft or fraud. For employers, it presents a holistic perspective on a candidate's reliability and accountability.

Typically, if an employer opts to conduct a credit check, it is typically towards the final stages of the hiring process, often after a decision to extend an offer has been made. Given the resource-intensive nature of credit inquiries, not all candidates will undergo this scrutiny, and it is primarily employed for roles involving financial responsibilities or positions where handling money is integral, such as accounting or retail positions.

Employers' Interest in Credit Checks

Employers conduct credit checks to safeguard their financial interests, workforce, and clientele by ensuring they hire individuals of integrity. They perceive credit checks as a means to glean insights into an applicant's character.

Credit history serves as a red flag for potential issues employers seek to avoid:

- Consistent late payments may suggest a lack of organization, responsibility, or adherence to agreements.
- High credit utilization or excessive debt indicates financial strain, which could heighten the risk of dishonest behavior such as theft or fraud.
- Instances of financial mismanagement might signal unsuitability for roles involving fiduciary responsibilities or handling consumer data.

According to a survey conducted by The Professional Background Screeners and HR.com in 2021, credit or financial checks are part of background screenings for 51% of U.S.-based companies.

Preparing for a Credit Check in Employment

Taking proactive steps to review your credit profile enables you to anticipate and rectify any erroneous negative entries beforehand. Utilize your entitlement to a complimentary credit report weekly from each of the three major bureaus through AnnualCreditReport.com. Rectify any inaccuracies through the dispute resolution process.

- Maintaining a healthy credit report is a prudent financial practice that also safeguards your credit score:
- Timely payment of bills is crucial, as payment history significantly influences credit scores and prevents delinquencies from tarnishing your record. Exercise restraint in utilizing available credit, ideally keeping balances below 30% of the available limit per card to demonstrate financial prudence and enhance credit scores.
- Regularly monitor your credit report using available resources such as NerdWallet to promptly address any adverse entries.

- Temporary lifting of credit freezes with major bureaus ahead of anticipated credit checks expedites the hiring process and prevents unnecessary delays.

Prepare to address any negative information in your credit reports transparently. Crafting explanations, such as detailing how a previous job loss contributed to a missed payment, demonstrates accountability to prospective employers.

Understanding Your Legal Protections

While it is true that your credit history can influence job opportunities, the Fair Credit Reporting Act (FCRA) provides safeguards for individuals. Below are the steps employers are required to follow under this legislation:

Notification and Consent: Employers must inform you if they intend to conduct a credit check and obtain your written consent. The FCRA mandates that this notification be clear, conspicuous, and separate from other communications.

Pre-Adverse Action Notice: If an employer is considering rejecting your application based on your credit report, they must notify you beforehand. This "pre-adverse action notice" should include a copy of the report and a summary of your rights.

Opportunity to Respond: You must be given a reasonable period, typically three to five business days, to address any concerns raised by the credit report. This allows you to explain any discrepancies or errors to the employer.

Post-Adverse Action Notice: Following any adverse decision, the employer must provide a post-adverse action notice. This notice should include details of the credit reporting agency used, their contact information, and your right to request a free copy of the report within 60 days.

Controversy Surrounding Employer Credit Checks

Critics argue that credit checks are irrelevant to job performance and can disproportionately impact minority job seekers, exacerbating economic inequalities. Chi Chi Wu, a senior attorney at the National Consumer Law Center, highlights racial disparities in credit scores, attributing them to factors such as the racial wealth gap and systemic discrimination.

To address these concerns, some states have imposed restrictions on employer credit checks. You can consult your state labor department or local government to determine if such limitations apply in your area. Supporters of employer credit checks contend that they provide valuable insights into a candidate's financial responsibility and decision-making skills, which could affect their suitability for certain roles in the future.

In conclusion, this chapter delves into the advanced topics of credit management, exploring the intricate relationships between credit and personal dynamics, as well as its profound impact on employment opportunities and housing decisions. By understanding the implications of joint accounts, co-signing arrangements, divorce, and separation on credit scores, as well as the role of credit in employment screening, insurance premiums, and renting decisions, readers will be equipped with the knowledge and tools needed to navigate these complex aspects of credit management with confidence and resilience.

CONCLUSION

"Success is not final, failure is not fatal: It is the courage to continue that counts."

And here you are, at the closing pages of this book. You have journeyed through the twists and turns of the credit repair landscape, and I must say, your commitment to mastering your financial destiny is truly admirable.

As we bid adieu, let's take a moment to reflect on the invaluable wisdom you have gained. Through the pages of this book, you have not only learned the intricacies of credit repair but also unearthed the power that lies within your hands to shape your financial future.

We've navigated the labyrinth of credit scores, demystified the enigma of credit reports, and dissected the art of rebuilding credit with patience and persistence. Together, we've uncovered the significance of setting up credit monitoring as a guardian of your financial fortress, ensuring that no lurking threat goes unnoticed.

Moreover, we've ingrained the importance of maintaining good credit practices into the fabric of your financial habits. From the timely payment of bills to the prudent management of credit card balances, you have armed yourself with the tools to wield credit as a force for prosperity.

But perhaps most importantly, we've discussed the pivotal moment when seeking professional credit repair help becomes not just an option, but a beacon of hope amidst the stormy seas of financial adversity. When confusion reigns supreme and progress seems elusive, remember that there are experts ready and willing to guide you back onto the path of financial enlightenment.

As you close this chapter of your journey, know that your quest for financial freedom is far from over. It isa lifelong expedition, filled with challenges and triumphs, setbacks and successes. But armed with the knowledge and resilience you have cultivated; I have every confidence that you will navigate this journey with grace and determination.

So, my friend, as you turn the final page of this book, remember this: you hold the pen to your financial story. Embrace the challenges, celebrate the victories, and never forget the power that lies within you to craft the life of your dreams.

Here is to your fresh start and the limitless possibilities that lie ahead!

GLOSSARY

FICO Score: A credit scoring model developed by the Fair Isaac Corporation (FICO) that is widely used by lenders to assess an individual's credit risk. FICO scores range from 300 to 850

Vantage Score: Another credit scoring model used by lenders to evaluate creditworthiness. Vantage Scores range from 300 to 850

FCRA (Fair Credit Reporting Act): A federal law that regulates the collection, accuracy, and dissemination of consumer credit information.

APR (Annual Percentage Rate): The annualized interest rate charged on a loan or credit card, expressed as a percentage of the principal amount. The APR reflects not only the interest rate but also any fees or charges associated with the loan, making it a more accurate measure of the true cost of borrowing.

Credit Report: A detailed record of an individual's credit history, including information about credit accounts, payment history, outstanding balances, credit inquiries, and public records

Credit Score: A numerical representation of an individual's creditworthiness, based on information in their credit report.

Credit Utilization: The ratio of credit card balances to credit limits, expressed as a percentage.

Credit Limit: The maximum amount of credit that a lender is willing to extend to a borrower on a credit card or line of credit.

Credit Monitoring: The practice of regularly reviewing one's credit reports and credit scores for changes or discrepancies.

Credit Freeze: A security measure that restricts access to an individual's credit report, making it more difficult for identity thieves to open new accounts in their name.

Credit Inquiry: A record of a lender's request for an individual's credit report or credit score.

Debt-to-Income Ratio (DTI): A financial metric that compares an individual's monthly debt payments to their gross monthly income.

Minimum Payment: The smallest amount of money that a borrower is required to pay toward their outstanding balance on a loan or credit card each billing cycle.

Interest Rate: The percentage of a loan or credit card balance that is charged as interest over a specified period.

Balance Transfer: The process of transferring an existing credit card balance to another credit card, typically with a lower interest rate or promotional terms.

Secured Credit Card: A type of credit card that requires a cash deposit as collateral, typically equal to the credit limit.

Unsecured Credit Card: A type of credit card that does not require collateral and is based solely on the borrower's creditworthiness.

Credit Counseling: Financial counseling services are provided by nonprofit organizations to help individuals manage debt, budget effectively, and improve their financial literacy.

Made in the USA
Monee, IL
04 November 2026

67386628R00066